REAL ES

BEST

KEPT SECRET

The FHA 203k Program Can Change Your Life and Financial Future!

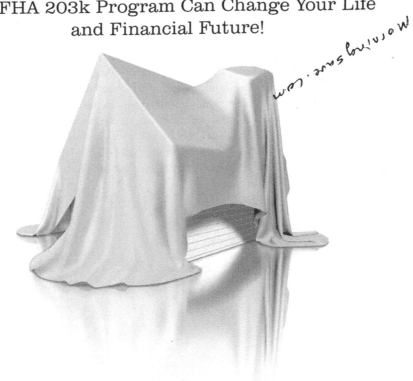

DENNIS and TERESA WALSH

DWA

Published by Dennis Walsh & Associates, Inc., Newport Beach, CA
Visit our website at www.rebuildusa.com.

Book Front Cover Design by Daniel Walsh
Book Rear Cover and Interior Design by Susanne Dwyer

ISBN-13: 978-0-9895252-0-6
Printed in the United States of America
First Edition: (June 15, 2013)
10 9 8 7 6 5 4 3 2 1

Dedication

This book is dedicated to our parents, who inspired us to believe in the power of the American Dream by achieving theirs with persistence, integrity and an unwavering belief in a higher purpose. We also dedicate this to our amazing, talented (and just a little crazy) children: sons Daniel and Christian, daughter-in-law Stephanie, and grandchildren Bella, Logan, Liam and Gianna, who bring great joy to our lives each and every day.

Author Bios

Dennis & Teresa Walsh founded Dennis Walsh & Associates, Inc. (DWA), the parent company of REbuildUSA, in 1988. Since that time, DWA has been in the business of delivering cutting-edge education and consulting to the world's leading real estate organizations.

Dennis and Teresa Walsh are respected for their innovation and contributions to America's housing industry and enjoy long-standing relationships developed over two decades of speaking, consulting and participating in events from coast to coast. As national FHA 203k experts, the Walsh's have been featured speakers at hundreds of conventions and live events on the subject.

Prior to DWA, both were active in a number of areas of construction and real estate. Dennis grew up working on construction sites, learning each of the building trades hands on, and eventually became a designer and builder of custom homes and major remodeling projects. He also owned and operated a factory-built housing, lumber and materials supply business, providing panelized building packages for projects throughout the eastern U.S.

Teresa worked in banking and earned her real estate license before taking on an ownership and management role in her family's marble, tile, stone and flooring business. In this capacity, she worked with architects, interior designers, material suppliers, builders and homeowners through various phases of the design, planning and construction process.

Based on their extensive experience in residential real estate and construction, the Walsh's recognized a unique opportunity to help consumers and real estate professionals tap into the power of the U.S. Government FHA 203k Renovation Loan program. To this end, REbuildUSA™ was established to help open up homeownership to many more Americans, while bringing new business to lenders, real estate professionals and the home renovation industry. REbuildUSA continues to grow its national membership, which currently includes thousands of 203k Specialist real estate and mortgage professionals throughout the nation.

Presented to more than 150,000 real estate professionals throughout the U.S., Canada and beyond, DWA's live presentations, webinars and designation courses, 203k Specialist (203KS), Certified New Home Specialist™ (CNHS) and Residential Construction Certified™ (RCC), are respected as the very best of their kind. Presented in computer-based, self-study format, these courses are endorsed and/or private-labeled by a "who's who" of real estate's leading organizations.

Prologue

It's September, 2006. My wife Teresa and I are walking through the lobby of the historic Roosevelt Hotel located right in the heart of midtown Manhattan. Surrounded by art and architecture of the 1920's, we're moving through a group of more than a thousand attendees at one of the real estate industry's premier events, the RISMedia Annual Leadership Conference. Everywhere we look are familiar faces—a "who's who" of real estate, including executives of the nation's largest brokerages, lenders and franchise systems, top speakers, consultants and other leaders of the industry.

Amid the conversation and laughter, attendees are studying conference guides to determine which of the late-morning sessions they're going to attend. Like almost everyone else shuffling by, our explorer skills are put to the test as we search for the location of the room for our next session. After navigating our winding course and turning the last corner, a sign greets us next to the door:

The Remodeling Boom is Here! –
Should You Be Remodeling Your Business?

Moderator: Dennis Walsh

As we set up our computer for the presentation, Teresa and I are excited about the fact that we're delivering a very different presentation this year. Having traveled the nation already for more than 16 years as nationally recognized speakers and trainers, our focus prior to this had always been residential construction and new-home sales and marketing.

As we built our new-home sales training business, we traveled extensively, always happy for the opportunity to share our message with any audience of real estate agents we could find. When we started, the level of cooperation between builders and REALTORS® was very low. In many areas of the country, the two groups felt they simply had no use for each other. Our mission initially was to share the message that there was a great deal to be gained when builders, developers and RE-

ALTORS® worked together effectively. REALTORS® could help builders identify the right locations and homes to build, while leveraging the power of their real estate marketing skills and resources. Builders could offer REALTORS® an ongoing source of inventory for sale—even customizing that inventory to better meet the needs of buyers. In the process, not only did builders and REALTORS® benefit, but the homebuyers as well.

Although our goal at that time was to provide the training, systems and marketing tools to support this business, in our first years, we felt like evangelists as we traveled from town to town sharing this new religion. One day led to the next, another town, another audience, and eventually we had delivered our training and shared our message with more than one hundred thousand real estate professionals throughout the nation and beyond. Our *Certified New Home Specialist and Residential Construction Certified* designation courses grew to become the most popular training of their kind in real estate.

But today is different. For this presentation, we had assembled a panel of experts to discuss a very new topic—not only for ourselves—but for the real estate industry as well. Teresa and I had been discussing this new direction for several years already. We felt strongly that there was a need for real estate professionals to begin to think differently about their role in the real estate transaction. In the session description, I wrote:

> With new development moving further from urban centers, more prospective buyers will look to older neighborhoods to meet their housing and lifestyle needs. More sellers will look for ways to position their homes for greater sales potential.
>
> How do we redefine our role to bring greater value to these transactions? Further, how does the brokerage of tomorrow move beyond its role in the sales transaction to become central to the total homeownership experience? This session explores the trends, challenges, opportunities and issues impacting real estate professionals as more sellers, buyers and homeowners seek home improvement guidance and services.

Most real estate agents concentrate their efforts on finding homes currently available for purchase that offer the best combination of location and desired features within the buyer's budget. And this makes sense. However, most agents are evaluating properties *as they sit.* In other words, they're looking for homes that are *move-in-ready* and offer as much as possible to meet the needs of their clients.

Having grown up in construction, and having spent many years teaching new-home sales strategies and skills, we saw that an alternative perspective could be highly valuable. Rather than focusing on only move-in-ready homes, why not also identify other homes that might actually be better choices if only they were updated and remodeled to meet buyers' needs? Think about how many great older homes, in great older neighborhoods, could ultimately give buyers more of what they really want for their money?

In fact, these older homes in need of a little love are typically available at prices that are discounted to reflect this need for repair and updating. If real estate professionals were to bring the solutions and support to help people in this way, they could be helping people to truly get more of the house they want for their money.

*Rather than paying a premium for a move-in-ready home that includes the value of changes made by the previous owners, wouldn't it make more sense to spend less on the home itself and invest in the actual improvements **these buyers** value most?*

Many sellers speak of "improvements" they've made, but unless those new cabinets, colors, finishes, etc., are equally valued by the buyer, those so-called improvements are instead really just changes. Yet, as all real estate professionals know, most sellers typically expect to recover the costs of all the changes they've made, regardless of how much they really "improve" the property.

As I quickly ran through my notes for the session, I reviewed statistics supporting our concept. The home remodeling industry had enjoyed a record year in 2005 with more than $280B in sales volume, with significant growth expected to continue. Our nation's housing stock in 2006 totaled roughly 120 million homes with a median age of 32 years. This presented a massive inventory of homes that would benefit from repair and renovation.

Further, with more anti-growth sentiment and increasing fees tied to land development and new-home building, as well as limited land availability close to urban centers, there were increasing incentives for people to remodel their existing homes. These same market conditions also created incentives for homebuyers to consider purchasing older homes in established neighborhoods. Many of these homes offer more desirable locations, larger yards and other benefits. And all of these changing needs were clearly pointing to new opportunities for real estate agents, brokerages, lenders and others in the industry.

Our esteemed panelists now began arriving for the session. Teresa greeted them at the door and helped them get situated at the front of the room. Checking my watch, I realized that our presentation was scheduled to begin in about five minutes. Yet only a handful of conference attendees had entered our room.

As I waited a few more minutes to begin the session, I thought back to what had inspired Teresa and me to start our journey down this road less traveled. As our training business grew, we spent literally thousands of days on the road. Our travels took us to almost every corner of this amazing country, and in the process, allowed us to enjoy many fantastic experiences and adventures.

As we admired so much of what this nation offers, from the beauty of nature to the great cities and other amazing achievements of the American people, we were also moved by the stark contrast found in so many older neighborhoods that were, in effect, dead or dying. Communities filled with homes that once stood proud and beautiful, were now falling apart, ridden with poverty and crime. Parks, churches, schools and shops that were once filled with life, now sit in despair, barely a shadow of what they had been so many years ago. And right in the heart of these dying neighborhoods, we would see people and families struggling to make a meaningful life. In these sad streets, children play. But unlike their counterparts in the nicer parts of town, these young people often grow up with less hope for their future. They struggle for survival in an environment of hopelessness. And this sad story plays over and over again across our nation, and will continue if this pattern is not somehow broken.

As we continued to see these decaying neighborhoods in our travels, Teresa and I would often talk about finding solutions. There are certainly many great organizations already working to overcome these challenges. But we also felt a dramatic difference could be made if our industry would step up and make a contribution as well. What if the housing industry could make it a mission to preserve and protect the very foundation that supports it? Was it possible to find a way to engage the people who build their careers around housing to play a more substantial role in preserving and rebuilding homes and communities? If so, could we also then work together preserving and rebuilding the lives of those who live there?

The key to this, we decided, was to do exactly what we had done for so many years in our new-home sales business. We would be putting on our evangelist hats once again to convince the industry that this was something important for them to do—and that in the process, they would enjoy greater success in their careers as well. We needed to show them that being a good citizen was also good for business. So here we were in New York City taking our first step to bring this dream to life.

At the top of the hour, as I stepped up to the podium to begin the introductions, I looked out over several hundred empty chairs with only a dozen or so people scattered here and there. I was used to presenting to rooms packed with people, sometimes lined up in the aisles and out the doors, but today was clearly different. Apparently more than a thousand conference attendees had decided that another session was more important or interesting. Discouraging to say the least, but the show must go on. And so it did.

Our panelists were excellent. As each of them shared their perspectives and interacted with our small audience, it was apparent we were on to something very important. Together, they built a strong case to support our message and the opportunities to be found. The attendees became engaged and, as conversation continued, there was a genuine excitement building in the room. Although our low attendance was undeniable evidence that we were far ahead of the curve on this, we all agreed that day that we were on the track of something very important.

My life experience had already taught me that many of the greatest ideas are not necessarily recognized for what they are. In fact, they're often the least obvious to those who are already engaged in a different way of doing things. History has shown us again and again that many of the world's greatest achievements come about only due to the determination of people who refuse to give up in the face of serious obstacles and non-believers. In spite of the lack of interest in our message that day, Teresa and I were even more determined to rally the industry behind this cause.

Of course, as the old adage says, "It's all about timing," so several more years passed as we kept the fires of this dream slowly burning.

Fast forward to October 2010. At a convention center in Dallas, Texas, an audience of more than 2,000 real estate brokers and agents surround a massive stage. Tami Bonnell, the President of Exit Realty, U.S., crosses the stage with her image projected behind her on two giant screens. The high energy music begins to fade as the crowd jumps to their feet, wild with applause to greet Tami, one of the most respected individuals in the industry. Having reached the podium, she waits for the noise to die down and begins her introduction:

> "This couple I'm introducing next, I've had the privilege of getting to know over the last few years. They work unbelievably hard, they're incredibly dedicated to adding value to communities, and absolutely dedicated to adding value to your lives. Ladies and gentlemen, let's give a warm welcome to Dennis and Teresa Walsh from REbuildUSA."

As we walked up onto the stage surrounded by the thunderous applause of those 2,000 people, I remembered back to that almost empty room in New York City. As they rose to their feet in a standing ovation at the end of our presentation, we were experiencing the power of a dream. This is what can be done through passion and determination.

For the next several years, we traveled the nation speaking to many thousands of people. And we're honored to say that REbuildUSA quickly grew to a national network of thousands of real estate and mortgage professionals dedicated to helping more Americans achieve the dream of homeownership through the power of the FHA 203k and other renovation loans.

Through this book and the support of REbuildUSA, Teresa and I hope our dream will truly help you and many others realize yours. Together, let's work to rebuild America, one home and one dream at a time.

Acknowledgements

As we put the final touches on "Real Estate's Best Kept Secret," Teresa and I are honored to think of the many wonderful people who played some meaningful part in the lifelong journey that brought us to this place. This book, and REbuildUSA, would simply not exist without the wisdom, support, inspiration and love given so generously by family, friends and business associates. Although a complete list would require its own chapter, we'd like to give special thanks to:

Brian Caine, Marisa Caine, Jenny Vita and Clyde Sedgwick, our fearless REbuildUSA leadership who work hard every day to keep things running smoothly and support us as we spread the 203k gospel across the nation.

Our son Daniel Walsh for his very cool cover design and Susanne Dwyer, who applied her special skills in editing, graphic design, proofreading and just plain awesomeness.

Our great friends, real estate experts, and very cool people: Steve Ozonian, Bryan Schutjer, Randy Purcell, John Featherston, Darryl MacPherson, David Schoner, K.C Chermak, Brian Jones, Howard Bobrow, Mike Dosen, Melody Bohrer, Nina Cotrell, Toni Sherman and our mentor David Horowitz and his lovely wife Maxine, all of whom generously share their wisdom and support our adventures.

John Adams, John Sway, Jim Ragan, Joe Daly, Sean Thompson, Chris Moore, Ron Bergum, Danny Zoller, Judy Weisman and other REbuildUSA partners who represent the best-of-the-best in the world of renovation lending.

Alex Perriello and our friends at Realogy, Dave Liniger, Mike Ryan and the entire RE/MAX gang, Ron and Arlie Peltier, Gino Blefari, Ed and Kathy Krafchow, Rei Mesa and Tami Bonell, as well as the thousands of real estate and mortgage professionals who make up our REbuildUSA network of 203k Specialists.

Lisa Ellis and Trish McBarren, the FHA's dynamic duo who generously share their knowledge and work so very hard to support the success of the 203k and EEM programs on a national basis.

Ken Jenny, Jamie Moyle and the amazing RealtyTrac team for everything they do in partnership with REbuildUSA to help more Americans enjoy the benefits of renovation loans.

The great folks at Lowe's who partnered with us to bring REbuildUSA to life, including Mark Malone, Lawrence Lobpries, David Kratt Nick Mraz, Tom Lamb, Michelle Deatherage, Donna Robinson, Len Sadek, Robert Wagner, Jeff Starnes and many others.

And finally, we thank our family, including Irene "Bomma" Rosati, Dan and Marianne Walsh, Jim and Marie Jones, Pat and Paula Walsh, Mark and Laura Walsh, Steve and Alexandra Dodds, Ray Rubio, Diane Rojas and Chris and Andrea Gialanella for their unconditional love and support.

Real Estate's Best Kept Secret
The FHA 203k Program Can Change Your Life and Financial Future!

Chapter 1

Opportunity of a Lifetime

Let's fast forward twenty or thirty years from today. You're surrounded by your children and grandchildren talking about how things used to be "back in the day." The conversation is about how dramatically things have changed in technology, travel, medicine and more. "I agree, things were really primitive back then," you say. "Cables everywhere, chargers left and right to keep batteries working. People actually driving cars themselves and using fax machines—and an iPad was considered sophisticated technology!"

The kids laugh as you share more examples of the funky old things you did back in the 2000s.

"There sure has been a lot of progress since then," you continue, "but I'll tell about something that was really fantastic back then—and provided an unbelievable opportunity that allowed us to buy our own home. We wouldn't be right here in this house today if it weren't for an amazing U.S. Government loan program. It was something that allowed millions of Americans to have their own shot at the American Dream."

Everyone nods as you explain further. "No one seemed to know this program even existed. We were fortunate enough to hear about it from some friends."

"So here's how it worked," you continue. "The mortgage would provide the money to buy a house and include additional money to fix it up. So funds for purchase and renovation are included all in one loan." You stop for a moment to let it sink in.

"What was great is that interest rates were really low at the time. And on top of that, you only had to come up with 3.5 percent for the down payment! I know it sounds crazy, but it's true. So that's how we were able to buy the home we're sitting in right now. We would never have been able to live in a home or neighborhood as nice as this otherwise."

"That's unbelievable," one of them says. "That opportunity literally changed your life...and ours, too."

"I can only imagine how many people are kicking themselves for not taking advantage of that loan program back then," says another.

"That's very true," you agree, "and as you know, this home is now worth many times more than what we paid for it back then, so it's turned out to be one of smartest financial moves we ever made."

Sounds pretty great, doesn't it? Is it possible you might be telling a similar story to your children and grandchildren someday? Is it possible the timing could be right for you to use the power of this little known government loan program to make one the best financial moves of your life?

Yes, it's absolutely possible! And for the most part, it's entirely up to you if you'd like to make this happen! Are you excited about that? I hope so. We're excited about helping you understand everything you need to know to make the most of this opportunity for yourself and your family.

All across America there are families and individuals right now bringing their dream of homeownership to life, leveraging the power of this great program. At the same time, there are many more who have no idea this opportunity exists. That's why we describe it as one of real estate's best kept secrets. And that's why we felt it was so important to dedicate ourselves to not only creating awareness, but helping to make this opportunity more easily available to as many people as possible.

I'm sure you'll agree that acting on this secret can truly change your life, both today and long into the future. Think about how this might change your financial future. Think about the impact this can have on your quality of life for many years. And think about the difference this might make for your children—and their children—some day.

So what is this best kept secret?

It's called the FHA 203k Renovation Loan, and it's considered by many to be the single most powerful opportunity available today for millions of Americans to realize the dream of homeownership.

"But I already own a home," some of you may be thinking. "Have I lost my chance to benefit from this program as well?"

Absolutely not! Here's another best kept secret:

The FHA 203k can also be used to refinance your existing home. You can refinance to take advantage of today's lower interest rates, and in the process, you can also add additional funds into this new mortgage to make repairs and other improvements.

So I ask again: Are you excited about this? I hope so. I also hope you become more excited as we move forward together in this book, helping you thoroughly understand this opportunity and how to make the very most of it for you and your family. As founders of REbuildUSA, Teresa and I have made it our business to learn as much as possible about the FHA 203k. We work every day with our support team and our network of thousands of mortgage and real estate 203k Specialists from coast to coast—and we've learned a lot in the process. In this book, we'll share information and strategies—more best kept secrets, if you will—that come from real-world experience supporting many thousands of successful 203k renovation loans.

So why are we doing this? Are we simply on a mission to help as many people as possible get a fantastic deal on a home? Well, yes— helping more people move into homeownership is certainly one of our most important goals. We also want to help folks who already own a home protect their investment and increase the quality of their life as well. But as you might imagine, there are some other important reasons we've dedicated our lives to this cause. So here's another secret:

Along with many others throughout the housing industry, we believe helping more Americans effectively use the FHA 203k Renovation Loan program will have a profound, positive impact on America in numerous ways.

Here are some of them:

▶ Through homeownership, more Americans enjoy the long-term investment benefits that contribute to their financial future.

▶ Increasing homeownership has a positive impact on communities across America, both financially and socially.

- Improving homes and neighborhoods reduces the spread of crime and poverty, creating safer, more positive environments for the people who live there.

- Through energy-efficient home improvements, we help reduce America's energy dependence and reduce the negative environmental impact associated with energy production.

- The repair and home improvement work done through these renovation loans creates employment and income opportunities for the construction industry.

- The work done by real estate and mortgage professionals to support renovation loan business creates additional employment and income for them.

Most of all, the passion Teresa and I bring to this mission comes from our deep-rooted desire to make a better world for the children of our great nation. Numerous studies substantiate the reality that safe, clean neighborhoods create an environment that helps children perform better scholastically and socially. As a result, we build a stronger future for our children and a stronger nation in the process.

Our dream is to help rebuild homes, neighborhoods and careers, and create a more positive future for as many people as possible. As we say in our REbuildUSA tagline, ***"We're Rebuilding America One Dream at a Time."***

Thinking of what you've already learned about the power of the 203k, please consider these questions:

- Are you interested in learning how you could enjoy ownership of a new home that reflects your lifestyle and personal tastes without paying a premium for a home in "perfect" condition?

- Have you passed up buying a great home in a great location because you didn't know how to finance the repairs and improvements it might need?

- Have you considered the purchase of a fixer-upper to allow you to earn some "sweat equity" by coordinating repairs and remodeling to increase its value?

- Would you like to buy an older home for its character, quality construction or other reasons, but would like to make improvements to increase its energy efficiency and lower your costs of ownership?

- Would you enjoy an opportunity to own more home for your money? Would you like to own a home that better suits the needs of your family and your personal style?

If you answer "yes" to any of these questions, the information and ideas we're sharing with you in this book can help make this happen for you!

Before we move on in our adventures here together, I'd like to make you aware that there are other forms of renovation loans available in addition to the FHA 203k. Often referred to as "conventional" renovation loans, these alternatives offer different features that can be beneficial to certain types of buyers under certain types of circumstances. As the 203k offers the greatest range of possibilities for the greatest range of homebuyers and homeowners, we're going to focus our attention here. Once you have a solid understanding of the 203k, you'll find that, for the most part, the processes, details and strategies will be similar for these alternative mortgage products.

Before we dig more deeply into the specifics of the FHA 203k and renovation loan transactions, let's first take a quick look at the FHA and what it's all about.

Chapter 2

What Is the FHA?

So what exactly is the FHA? It seems a lot of people have heard of the FHA, but are not really sure what it's all about. The U.S. Federal Housing Administration was established all the way back in 1934 with the mission to improve housing conditions and homeownership opportunities throughout America. The FHA was originally created in the aftermath of the Great Depression to help get our economy back on track.

The following is what's written on the FHA website to describe circumstances at that time.

"When the FHA was created, the housing industry was flat on its back:

▸ Two million construction workers had lost their jobs.

▸ Terms were difficult to meet for homebuyers seeking mortgages.

▸ America was primarily a nation of renters. Only four in 10 households owned homes, so homeownership was only 40 percent at that time."

So what do you think? This certainly has a familiar ring to it, doesn't it? The FHA program, then, was originally created to help overcome economic conditions very similar to what we've experienced in our recent recessionary times.

Has the FHA been successful with its mission? Absolutely! Since its inception, various FHA loan programs have been used to finance more than 34 million homes, and that number is climbing quickly every year now.

And its impact reaches far beyond housing. By making it easier for Americans to buy homes, the FHA also helps create more jobs and income which stimulates the overall economy in many, many ways. With what we're facing today, it's not surprising the FHA is again having a big impact.

During the 1940s, the FHA played a major role in housing our active military and veterans. Years later, in 1965, the FHA was set up as a division under the management of HUD, which stands for "The Department of Housing and Urban Development," and still operates this way today. In addition to its impact on the overall economy through for-sales housing, FHA programs have also lead to the construction of many millions of apartments to meet the needs of the elderly, handicapped and lower-income Americans. I'm sure you'll agree that these are important contributions on many levels.

Now that you have an understanding of the purpose of the FHA, what exactly is an FHA Loan? You may have heard the terms "government guaranteed" or "FHA guaranteed."

What we refer to as an FHA "loan" is actually "loan insurance." In reality, the FHA doesn't actually provide mortgage funds, but instead provides loan insurance to lenders that protects them against losses in the event a homeowner were to default on the mortgage. This reduces the lenders' risk, allowing them to offer loans to buyers with less than perfect credit and requiring lower down payments. Lenders are also able to offer more competitive rates than they might not have been able to otherwise.

To qualify for this loan insurance, lenders must follow specific guidelines. Otherwise, they risk losing their FHA-approved lender status.

So what are the benefits of an FHA loan? The FHA offers the following:

▶ **Low Cost** – FHA-insured loans have competitive interest rates because the federal government insures the loans for lenders, reducing their risk.

▶ **Smaller Down Payment** – FHA-insured loans have a low 3.5 percent down payment and the money can come from a family member, employer or charitable organization as a gift.

▶ **Easier Qualification** – Because FHA insures your mortgage, lenders may be more willing to give you loan terms that make it easier for you to qualify.

▶ **Less than Perfect Credit** – You don't have to have perfect credit to get an FHA-insured mortgage. In fact, even if you have had credit problems, such as a bankruptcy, it's easier for you to qualify for an FHA-insured loan than a conventional loan.

▶ *FHA Loans Are Assumable* – What this means is that if you decide to sell your FHA-financed home at a later date, qualified buyers can "assume," or take over, the previous owner's loan instead of being required to get a brand new loan on their own. This becomes especially valuable if the seller has an interest rate on their FHA mortgage that's substantially lower than market rates at the time of sale.

▶ *More Protection to Keep Your Home* – The FHA has been helping people since 1934. Should you encounter hard times after buying your home, the FHA has many options to keep you in your home and avoid foreclosure.

I'm sure you'll agree these are some excellent benefits for a homebuyer. Another question that often comes up is: "How is the FHA funded? Do these programs place an additional burden or risk on American taxpayers?"

That's an excellent question and the answer is something else that's very cool. The FHA does not require massive allocations of taxpayer money to do what it does. In fact, its programs are entirely funded by proceeds generated from the loans it endorses. The money to fund FHA loans actually comes from the private markets. As a result, the FHA is the only government agency that is entirely self-funded—operating at no cost to the American taxpayers. Additionally, the home construction and community development driven by FHA programs stimulate the economy through job creation, tax revenues and more. As you can see, this is all very good stuff.

So where do these loan proceeds come from?

A mortgage insurance premium, commonly referred to as "M.I.P.," is included in the mortgage payments of all FHA loans. This is the "insurance premium," so to speak, that is charged to cover the operations of the FHA and supports a reserve fund to provide for reimbursement to lenders if a loan default occurs. This is the source of money that makes up the FHA Reserve Fund, which is what is used when lenders are reimbursed for a loan that goes into default.

Now, we can't talk about FHA loans without making sure you also understand something known as FHA loan limits. Since its inception, the FHA has set limits on the maximum amount of loan funds available to a borrower relative to housing costs in a given geographic area. In an area with lower-average home values, the FHA limits are lower. In areas where homes are more expensive, the limits are higher.

So another reason FHA loans were losing their luster during the housing boom was that the loan limits were not high enough to keep up with the crazy increases in home prices. Unless you were buying at the very bottom of the market, these limits were easily exceeded, leaving fewer and fewer homes that could qualify for use of FHA financing.

In an effort to help stimulate housing, the federal government then increased these limits to make FHA financing available to a broader segment of buyers. Currently, loan limits range from $271,000 to as high as $729,750. What this means is that even if your income and credit worthiness would allow you to afford a larger mortgage, your lender will not allow you to exceed the limits established for an FHA loan in your region. However, the current, higher loan limits open up the opportunity to apply both regular FHA loans and the 203k to a pretty large segment of our housing inventory. This explains another reason FHA loans have played such an important role in the nation's housing recovery.

If you'd like to find out what the current limits are for anywhere in the country, you can simply visit HUD's website at hud.gov and search for "FHA loan limits." You'll find a form allowing you to select a county, which will then show you the effective loan limits for your area.

So, I think you'll agree, in a nutshell—the FHA is pretty awesome— and an important key to helping more Americans make their dream of owning a nice home in a nice community come true.

Chapter 3

What Makes the FHA 203k Special?

So now that we've taken a quick look at FHA programs in general, let's get back to the hero of our story here—the FHA 203k renovation loan program. What is it that makes it so special?

The FHA 203k is a U.S. Government-guaranteed loan that provides funds for purchase or refinance, plus the cost of repairs and renovation packaged into a single mortgage loan.

Think about the possibilities. One loan to buy it and fix it up. Once the purchase of the home is closed exactly as it would be with a conventional loan, then renovation funds are set up in an escrow account to pay for pre-determined renovation work done by approved contractors.

As you're probably aware, the purchase of a house that needs repair is often a catch-22 situation because banks won't lend the money to buy the house until the repairs are complete, and the repairs can't be done until the house has been purchased. In this respect, another way to look at a 203k is that it's a mortgage loan that allows you to close on a home in disrepair. You simply can't get a conventional mortgage in place on a home that does not have a working HVAC system, or serious electrical issues, or a seriously damaged roof. More sellers today don't have the money to make these repairs themselves, and in the case of REO (homes owned by banks) homes coming back through foreclosure, most lenders prefer to sell these homes "as is."

We've talked about the many benefits of FHA financing, however, the normal non-renovation FHA mortgage loan—the 203b—requires a home inspection to assure the property meets HUD minimum code standards. If a home for sale requires more than $5,000 in repairs to meet these HUD code standards, a normal FHA mortgage loan can't be used to make the purchase.

Think about what's going on in today's market. How many homes for sale today, especially distressed properties, are in serious disrepair? You've seen it, or have at least heard the stories. An agent is touring a foreclosed home and gets a little confused trying to find the kitchen, because the entire kitchen is gone! Cabinets, countertops, appliances, even the light fixtures have somehow disappeared into thin air. Either the previous owner raised a little cash selling off parts of the house, or the neighbors snuck in and had a field day looting!

Homes like this are a perfect opportunity for using a 203k.

But it's not only homes coming back through foreclosure that create this opportunity. Many people, even many in the real estate and mortgage business, are not aware that 85 percent of all the homes in America were built before 1990. Today, this adds up to roughly 115 million homes that are more than 20 years old. Think about any 20-year-old home you've seen. Chances are it needs something in the way of repairs and improvements. More often, these homes need a lot of love!

As a result, it just makes sense that the 203k offers an excellent solution for buying almost any home. In fact, another important area in today's distressed market is the preponderance of short sales. These are homes sold by the homeowner at a price that's less than the current outstanding mortgage. Of course, this requires cooperation and approval by the primary lender and any other lien holders, but we find more and more homes going through this process in lieu of foreclosure. Like other distressed properties, these homes are often in need of repair. And of course, many buyers are interested in having additional changes and updates made as well. Again, the 203k comes to save the day.

Even in the case of homes that are being sold under more normal conditions, the renovation loan can be the ideal solution. When I ask real estate agents in my seminars, "How often do you show a home—any home—to a prospective buyer even if it's only a few years old, that the buyer feels is absolutely perfect as it sits?" The resounding answer is almost always: "Never!"

In almost every home purchase, regardless of how well it's been maintained, the new owners want to make changes of some kind. New appliances or flooring, new paint, maybe light fixtures, a new deck or patio, some built-ins—there's always something!

I'm sure you can see that the 203k and other renovation loans offer a very important solution—far more important than most people have realized. Although we'll go into more detail later on, here's a quick overview of some of the key benefits to potential homeowners:

▶ **Save Time and Money** – Use one loan to buy and renovate a great home to meet your needs.

▶ **Get More Home for Your Money** – Take advantage of the excellent prices for homes that need repair and remodeling to end up with a larger home or a better location than you might have otherwise.

▶ **Low Down Payment** – Enjoy the benefits of homeownership with as little as 3.5 percent down payment. These down payment funds can also be gifted by family, employer or a charity.

▶ **Easier Qualification** – Less strict FHA qualification requirements benefit those with less than perfect credit. Higher debt-to-income ratios help buyers qualify for a higher mortgage amount than most conventional loans.

▶ **Live in a More Desirable Location** – There are many great homes in wonderful, established neighborhoods that offer perfect FHA 203k opportunities.

▶ **Make the Most of Your Investment** – Rather than paying a premium for changes made by previous owners, invest in improvements that suit your personal tastes and lifestyle.

▶ **Earn Additional Equity** – Professional installers do the work and you can earn "sweat equity" in the process.

▶ **Greater Financial Stability** – Rather than experiencing a strain on your budget for major repairs later, you can pay for these improvements over time at a more affordable rate.

▶ **Invest in Your Future** – You can use an FHA 203k loan to purchase a one- to four-unit property, allowing you to renovate a home that also brings you rental income as an excellent long-term investment.

I'm sure you agree that these are powerful benefits that many Americans would want to enjoy. Yet, even though this loan program has been available since 1978, there has been very little awareness and very little use of this wonderful solution.

Chapter 4

Why a Best Kept Secret?

Back in 2009, as we were building REbuildUSA, I remember reaching out on the phone to a number of the most respected executives in real estate and mortgage and talking with them about our program to simplify the use of FHA 203k's. One after another told me they had never heard of it.

"When you first said the term '203k'," explained the CEO of a large, national real estate organization, "I thought you were talking about all that's left of my 401k in this lousy economy!" Over the last few years alone, I've met thousands of real estate agents who had never heard of a 203k, nor had any idea what it was. So don't let it bother you if you haven't heard of it—you're in some pretty good company.

When you explore things further, you find there are a number of good reasons behind the lack of awareness and lack of use of this amazing financial option.

One reason behind this can be explained by the fact that you don't find any marketing award trophies on the mantle of the White House. The U.S. Government is simply not known for its clever and creative marketing prowess. I think it's a safe bet that no one from Madison Avenue had a seat at the 203k planning committee table. The good folks at HUD clearly built an amazing program to benefit many potential homebuyers and current owners, but driving awareness of the existence of the product and its many benefits just hasn't been a priority.

Another reason behind so little use of the 203k and other FHA loans for quite a few years is the fact that low-interest and no-money-down mortgage loan alternatives were plentiful. Why bother with an FHA loan if you can more easily get a first and second mortgage to finance your home, improvements, new toys, vacations and more? On top of that, almost anyone could qualify for a mortgage in the height of the housing boom/bubble. You didn't need proof of a job, proof of income or hardly proof of anything that might indicate that you could actually pay the mortgage. Things got so out of hand, it appeared at one point that if you could fog a mirror, you were a prime candidate to buy a home! And as we know all too well, it's that kind of insanity that brought down the house, pun intended, a few years later. Sadly, we'll still be paying for the cleanup of that big mess for many years.

So money was easy and plentiful, regardless of whether you could really afford it, without requiring the support of the FHA. For example, in the year 2005, when an annual record of more than 7 million existing home sales were reported, less than 3 percent of all mortgage loans were endorsed by the FHA. As one top industry executive put it, "Most real estate agents didn't even know how to spell 'FHA' during the boom years."

As the market turned, however, we saw a dramatic shift in this thinking. Sub-prime, low down payment, interest-only, and easy qualification loans disappeared almost overnight when the economy hit the skids. As a result, the use of FHA financing became the only game in town for many buyers, driving the use of FHA-endorsed loans to record-setting levels.

Focusing specifically on the 203k, another reason we saw such little use is that most lenders and real estate professionals simply did not understand them or know how to support them. For those who did have at least an understanding, many found them to be far too challenging to close within a reasonable time frame. There's no question that there are more moving parts in the process of closing a renovation loan when compared to a conventional mortgage.

One factor contributing to this lack of understanding was the fact that very little was available in the way of training, so becoming truly knowledgeable about the 203k was not an easy task. You could sort through a mountain of information on the HUD website, but not too many people I know would have come back out of that experience alive. Honestly, if you feel you are absolutely so bored, that you could not possibly become more bored, I have a way to get you there. Just go online, navigate to hud.gov, and dig through all the information you can find there about the 203k. Not only will you become bored beyond belief, you might wake up one day in a daze, wondering where the last six months of your life have gone!

If you did attempt to tackle this, after reading all the overview and FAQ pages about the 203k, you would next download the 203k Handbook, affectionately known as "4240.4 Revision 2." This latest revision of this masterpiece was done in 1991, giving us a 100-page snapshot of the program as it stood more than 20 years ago. To bring you up to date, you would then very carefully study a series of what the FHA calls "Mortgagee Letters," each of which is an addendum to the latest handbook or most recent mortgagee letters, highlighting changes and updates to the program. It's not unusual to find numerous topics and regulation changes in each letter. Studying the current list, I find a total of 35 mortgagee letters that must be reviewed to fully understand the nuances of complying with FHA guidelines in the process of bringing a 203k mortgage to life. Doesn't that sound like fun?

Now if that actually does sound like fun to you, not only must you be really bored already, I could have used your help many years ago when I tackled this project!

As you can imagine, going through this learning process to truly understand the 203k was not only extremely challenging for lenders and REALTORS®, but even more confusing for a prospective homebuyer. As a result, many found this option to be simply too overwhelming to comprehend, let alone attempt to pursue.

The good news is that today, you don't have to go through this agony. We've already done the suffering for you. Just as we sorted through the confusion to create comprehensive training for the professionals, here in this book we're sharing the details, information and strategies you need to know as a homeowner or buyer.

So here we have a powerful solution that could benefit millions of homebuyers every year, and additional millions of current homeowners, yet the combination of factors discussed above has kept the 203k almost unknown to consumers. So unknown, in fact, that as the U.S. housing industry set a new record with more than 7 million existing home sales in 2006, less than 3,000 203k loans were endorsed by the FHA!

What's great today is that we're now seeing tremendous growth in this awareness. Looking back to May 2009, a Google search for "FHA

203k" turned up less than 100 hits outside of the official HUD web-site. Today, this same search returns almost one million results!

So here you are on the ground floor of a great "new" opportunity, learning about a way of financing your home that many of us believe will quickly grow to be the solution of choice for millions of Americans every year. To continue our journey together, let's next take a deeper dive into understanding some of the specifics of 203k loans as well as the types of homeowners allowed to benefit from this program.

Chapter 5

General 203k Guidelines

I n the following sections, we're going to explore 203k loans in much more detail. Before diving in, however, I'd like to emphasize an important "golden rule" I share with real estate professionals as well, and that is: *Your lender is your quarterback!*

The FHA lays down specific regulations and guidelines that must be followed in the process of approving, underwriting and finalizing 203k loans. It's up to your lender to understand these requirements and manage the overall process to assure conformance. It's very important that the lender does this job effectively, because it's essential that all the "t's" are crossed and all the "i's" are dotted if the lender were to come back to the FHA to honor a claim. Further, the lender's approved status with the FHA depends on its consistent conformance with these rules.

Another important point is that even though the FHA establishes minimum standards, in certain areas, *the lender has the option to be more restrictive*. For example, the FHA establishes a minimum credit score, but a lender may instead require a slightly higher score.

So again, your lender is your quarterback—and that's a good thing. We'll talk about this more as we go, offering you advice so you can make the most of this reality.

To get started on a better understanding of the specifics of the FHA 203k program, let's run down a list of some initial key points together.

▶ *Eligible 203k Properties* – The 203k can be used for purchase or refinance and renovation of one- to four-unit residential properties, mixed-use properties and condos. One caveat is that the home must have had an occupancy permit in place for a minimum of one year. In other words, we cannot use a 203k to purchase a brand new home that was not completed to at least the point where it passed a final inspection and was issued an actual certificate of occupancy. Later on in this book, we'll go into more detail on FHA regulations as it relates to the different types of eligible properties identified above.

▶ *FHA 203k Is a Single Close Loan* – As discussed earlier, the 203k is a single mortgage loan that provides funds for both the purchase of a home as it sits, as well as funds for renovation. These are packaged together in what is known as a "single close" loan, as opposed to using a combination of two separate loans to achieve the same end. The benefits to you include a simpler process and less paperwork, as well as cost savings since the duplication of various fees is eliminated with a single close.

▶ *Purchase Funds Paid at Closing* – When the closing occurs, the funds are released for payment of the home as it sits, exactly as it's done on a conventional mortgage loan. So we are now taking ownership of the home.

▶ *Renovation Funds Put in Escrow* – Unlike a conventional mortgage, we also have some amount of funds that have been allocated for repairs and improvements. These funds are commonly referred to as the renovation funds, and are now, at closing, set up in an account known as the "renovation escrow account." Managed by the lender similar to what is done with a new construction loan, the funds are then released during the renovation phase of the project based on a draw process, which varies depending on the type of project as well as the type of 203k loan we're using.

▶ *Maximum Six Months Allowed for Renovation* – The FHA allows for a maximum renovation period of six months, regardless of the scope of the project. As you would expect, many less complicated projects will not require the total six months. In fact, many 203k renovations are completed in less than 30 days. On the other hand, it is important to consider this time limitation if we're looking to tackle a complicated, large-scale renovation.

▶ *Multiple Contractors Allowed* – The point here is that we are allowed to contract the project using more than one contractor. Although the majority of people will prefer to have one company working in the capacity of a general contractor, the flexibility to hire an additional contractor or two, especially for certain highly specialized trades, can be beneficial.

▶ *Self-Help Arrangement* – This is the term the FHA uses to describe the opportunity for the homeowner to participate in doing portions of the renovation work themselves. As you might imagine, the interest in doing this comes up quite a bit as people look for opportunities to save money on the cost of the project.

They may have an interest in doing some painting, installing some flooring or other similar activities.

Current FHA guidelines tell us this is allowable, but only if the homeowner can demonstrate professional-level skills and experience in this type of work. For example, to install light fixtures, the homeowner would be required to establish both experience and licensing as a professional electrician. As you would expect, this limits the number of homeowners who ultimately are able to consider this option.

Even in a situation where the homeowner is qualified, they can only be reimbursed for the materials portion of the installation. There is no reimbursement for labor. Additionally, the lender is required to maintain additional back-up funds in the renovation escrow account for both material and labor in case the homeowner is not able to successfully complete the work. As you might guess, considering the fact that lenders can choose to be more restrictive than the FHA's minimum guidelines, it's not unusual to find lenders who simply do not allow use of the self-help arrangement under any circumstances.

▶ *No "Cost-Plus" or "T&M" Contracts* - Prior to the close of the loan, the FHA requires a scope of work clearly defining the details of the work to be completed and the products, materials and fixtures to be used. Along with this, complete total price must be established in writing in the form of a contract between the homeowner and the chosen contractor.

As a result, Cost-Plus or Time & Materials contracts are not allowed. If you are not familiar, these approaches both involve the contractor charging the actual costs of the work done, plus an additional fee calculated as a percentage of these costs added for management services. For any renovation loan, firm pricing must be established up front and finalized in a written contract. This is used as a basis for the appraisal, is required for closing and then serves to guide the distribution of renovation escrow funds as the project is completed.

▶ *Identity of Interest* – This term refers to a personal or business relationship that exists between parties of a home purchase contract. In its normal lending, FHA requires these relationships are identified, and depending on the nature of the relationship between a buyer and seller, there may be a larger down payment requirement. In the case of the 203k, identity of interest concerns go even further. The FHA does not want to see personal or direct business relationships existing between the various parties. The contractor, for example, cannot have a family or close personal relationship to the REALTOR®, lender or homebuyer. This is another example of an area where your lender will provide you guidance relative to your specific transaction.

Chapter 6

Eligible 203k Buyers

Next, let's identify who is eligible to participate in the 203k program as a buyer:

▶ *Owner-Occupants* – For the most part, the 203k is designed as a product targeted to owner-occupants. This means this mortgage is funding the ownership of a home used as a primary residence, occupied by the mortgagee, for a period of at least one year. Since this is allowed for only a primary residence, you can conclude that a 203k loan is not allowable on a second home or vacation home that is used only occasionally.

This also means that, typically, an individual is not allowed to have more than one FHA loan at any time. However, there is an exception to this that can be approved on a special request basis. This exception can be made in the case where someone works a job that would require them to split their time between two distant locations, in effect, requiring them to maintain two primary residences. To explore this possibility, again I emphasize that your lender is your quarterback. If you feel this might apply in your case, your lender can reach out on your behalf to the regional FHA Home Ownership Center, or "HOC," to make application for this variance.

▶ *U.S. Citizens and Resident Aliens* – When we talk about owner-occupants, the FHA allows this to apply to not only U.S. citizens, but also non-U.S. citizens who are residents here in the United States.

▶ *No Investors* – With a focus on owner-occupants, the FHA is not allowed to be used by investors for the purchase of properties for any other purpose other than their own primary residence. Now, if you spent time digging around hud.gov, studying all the information there related to the 203k program, you'll find quite a few references to use by investors. This is because investors were allowed to use the program when it was first introduced.

Unfortunately, there were problems that surfaced where some investors were abusing the program, creating additional risk exposure for the FHA. Eventually, in 1996, a moratorium was announced on use by investors and remains in place today.

There has been a great deal of interest and conversation around the idea of bringing back investor participation. In fact, many groups throughout the industry have expressed their wishes that HUD would reinstate investor use. With so many properties in need of renovation, many feel the 203k could play an even more substantial role in benefiting housing. If investor use is allowed at some time in the future, it's clear that very different guidelines and minimum requirements will be established for a newly designed "Investor K."

In the meantime, be aware that some of the alternative renovation loan products do allow options for investors. If you're interested in learning more about these opportunities, REbuildUSA can introduce you to lenders who specialize in these programs.

▶ *Non-Profits and Government Agencies* – This provision allows various groups dedicated to neighborhood revitalization to also take advantage of the benefits of the 203k. With so many distressed properties and blighted neighborhoods in urban areas, there are opportunities to leverage the 203k program to play a role in helping bring communities back to life. The availability of use by non-profits and government agencies is dependent on lenders' support of which we've seen little in recent years.

So that gives you a picture of the categories of eligible buyers from the perspective of the FHA, but what I'd like to do is now take a look at possible renovation loan buyers from another perspective. Let's explore the types of people who could enjoy the benefits of the 203k loan program in various ways. Do you fit into one of the following categories?

▶ *First-Time Buyers* – The benefits of a low down payment, as well as more flexible qualification clearly make regular FHA financing a popular solution for first-time buyers. With the 203k, we can take these benefits even further. If you are single, a couple or young family, you may be very excited about an opportunity to get a great deal on a fixer-upper. Not only does this offer the ability to customize the home to reflect your unique tastes, but it's a great way to earn some real equity, as improvements increase the appeal and value of the home.

▶ *Move-Up and Move-Down Buyers* – What we're talking about here are home-owners who are currently living in a home that's just not ideal for their needs. Maybe there's a baby on the way, or parents would like to move to an area with a school system they find more desirable for their children. Or maybe the kids are moving out and the house is just too big for these empty-nesters. Some people decide they need more room for a home office or an in-law suite, and it's just not practical or cost effective to remodel the existing home. For these, and many other reasons, the 203k offers an amazing solution for many who are looking for the most home for their money.

▶ *Those Who Desire an Urban Location* – In almost all areas of the country, there's been a steady migration of people heading back to the city—whether that city is large or small. If you are someone who would enjoy being closer to shopping, culture, work, or other activities and conveniences found in an urban center, you could find the 203k to be the perfect mortgage product to make that happen. Research makes it clear that the trend toward urban living is very real—especially for homeowners who just can't stand the many hours lost doing windshield time to and from work each day.

When you consider the many amazing older neighborhoods in great locations, and the homes there built with beautiful, old-world craftsmanship, I think you might find this appealing. Not only do these homes often have beautiful architectural detailing and character, they can be found at excellent prices. With some cosmetic updating and some energy-efficiency improvements, these become wonderful homes for many different types of homeowners and families.

▶ *Buyers Looking for Discounts and Sweat Equity* – Most of us are aware there are excellent deals available on homes in need of repair throughout the U.S., and many more to come. Once renovated, it's not unusual for these homes to appraise at a value that exceeds the total costs of the home purchase and added improvements. The challenge for most is that they're not aware of the FHA 203k program and believe the only way to enjoy these discount opportunities is through a cash purchase. I like to describe this as an opportunity to earn "sweat equity without the sweat" since we're utilizing professional contractors to do the actual renovation work.

Not only can you maximize your ability to earn equity by buying properties deeply discounted, but also by carefully analyzing the improvement you are making. This is where the expertise of a skilled real estate professional, lender and contractor can make a real difference. With their guidance, you can better identify those improvements that will have the greatest impact on the overall value of your new home.

▶ *Occupant-Investors on Multi-Family Properties* – This is another fantastic opportunity that's been a "best kept secret." The 203k can be used for the purchase of one- to four-unit residential properties and mixed-use properties—think about the possibilities here!

As long as we choose to live in one of the units as an owner-occupant, this option allows us to use a 203k loan to purchase and renovate a duplex, triplex or fourplex, and rent out the other units to bring in additional income. This also applies, as we said, to mixed-use properties, where we find residential units combined with retail or commercial space. I'm sure you'll recognize that these types of properties are found all across the country in both big towns and little towns. We're also finding many municipalities revising their zoning to allow mixed uses that support this opportunity. Small residential multi-unit properties have been a tried and true investment vehicle throughout history.

Here's another "secret" if you will: You can purchase and renovate a property with more than four units, as long as you end up with no more than four when the project is completed.

For example, you might find an excellent deal on a six- or seven-unit building that can be modified to have four larger units. The reason this can be an especially appealing option is found in the fact that a residential property with greater than four units requires commercial financing—which, for most people today, is almost impossible to secure with any kind of competitive terms. As a result, when someone desires to sell this type of property, the limited buyer pool can sometimes result in discounted acquisition prices.

▶ *Smart Buyers* – In my travels, I've shared the power of the FHA 203k and these specific areas of opportunity with many thousands of real estate and mortgage professionals. After covering the features and benefits of 203k's I've shared with you so far, I typically ask the audience how many of them would consider using a 203k if they themselves were in the market for a home today. The response is always the same. Almost every single hand goes up in the room.

Based on your much better understanding of the power of the 203k renovation loan program, would you agree that this presents opportunities that could make sense for you? Well, I hope you're excited about this. With this in mind, we're now going to dig even deeper to discuss the differences between Standard and Streamline versions of this amazing mortgage product.

Chapter 7

Comparing the Standard 203k and Streamline 203k

An aspect of the FHA 203k that often causes confusion is the fact that it comes in two popular flavors: the Standard and the Streamline. Let's make sure you have a clear understanding of the differences.

The Standard is the original version of the 203k which was introduced in 1978. This version is commonly referred to as the "Standard K," "Full K" or the "Consultant K," which we'll explain a little later on.

Many years later, the FHA decided there was a need for a new version that was less complicated for projects that were less complicated. In 2005, mortgagee letters 05-19 and 05-50 introduced the "Streamline 203k Limited Repair Program." This new version was intended to create an easier-to-use program that would apply to homes requiring non-structural improvements. The other major differentiator is that for use of the Streamline 203k, renovation costs and related expenses are not to exceed a total of $35,000. Folks in the industry refer to this version as the "Streamline K" or sometimes even the "Little K" or "Baby K."

What we're going to do next here is take a detailed look at the differences between these two versions. However, as we run through these details, I'd like to remind you again of the advice I shared earlier that your lender is your quarterback. Although it's helpful to understand the differences between these two types, ultimately, it's up to your lender to decide which makes the most sense for your particular situation. Once we review the differences, we'll discuss the logic behind this a little further.

To provide a handy reference, I've assembled a table here that contrasts the Standard and Streamline 203k's in a number of key areas.

Standard 203k	Streamline 203k
Maximum renovation to loan limit	$35,000 maximum renovation
Structural work allowed	No structural work allowed
Architectural/engineering required	No architectural/engineering
Landscaping/site improvements O.K.	No landscaping/site improvements
$5,000 minimum repairs	No minimum repairs
203k Consultant required	203k Consultant not required
Up to five draws	50% upfront draw + final draw
Inspections for each draw	Final inspection if more than $15,000
10% holdback required	Holdbacks not required
10% contingency reserve required	Contingency reserve optional
More eligible improvements	Fewer eligible improvements
More documentation	Less documentation
Up to six months PITI if not habitable	30 days maximum not habitable

Let's explore each of these differences:

▶ *Maximum Renovation to Loan Limit vs. $35,000 Maximum Renovation* – With a Standard K, there is no limit on the percentage or the total dollar amount that can be dedicated to the renovation portion of the loan, as long as the total loan does not exceed the applicable FHA loan limits for the area, and the appraised value of property following completion of the improvements. In an extreme example, let's say you qualified for a $300,000 loan and you found a property that you could purchase for only $10,000. As long as the appraisal would support the investment, you could theoretically borrow $290,000 for repairs and improvements. I'm sure you'll agree that this example is pretty unlikely to happen, but it illustrates the flexibility of the loan.

A Streamline 203k, on the other hand, is limited to a maximum of $35,000 in funds to be used for renovation purposes. As you can imagine, this can become a limiting factor pretty quickly when we're working with a property that needs any substantial amount of work. It's not unusual for a major kitchen remodel alone to put us over the top on this amount.

It's also important to keep in mind that there are additional costs related to the 203k that are typically included in the renovation funds amount. This can include the costs of inspections, permits and other applicable fees. On top of this, most lenders will require a contingency amount, which we'll discuss in a few minutes. What this means is that after these amounts, the funds available for actual renovation labor and materials on a Streamline often fall in the range of about $30,000-$31,000. Your lender will be happy to provide a breakdown on this for you.

▶ **Structural Work Allowed vs. No Structural Work Allowed** – This is one of the most significant differentiators you'll find between these two products. Most people are amazed to learn how much can be done with a Standard K. There are very few limitations. We can build a room addition, raise a roof, move walls and make any other kinds of structural changes. As an extreme example, let's say a home has been destroyed by a tornado or fire. As long as there is a foundation in place, we can use a Standard 203k to literally rebuild a home from the ground up.

The Streamline K, however, does not allow any structural activities at all. Regardless of the amount of work to be done, even if the total costs are well below the $35,000 limit, we are required to use the Standard version if there's anything on the project that's considered structural work.

I think you can see where this can cause some challenges as well. Let's say we have a home that appears to easily fall within the Streamline guidelines, but at some point it's discovered that termite damage has occurred and floor joists or rafters or some other structural components must be replaced. Even though we may have already started down the path of using a Streamline, once we find a requirement for structural repairs, we must now switch gears and move forward on this loan as a Standard.

▶ **Architectural/Engineering Required vs. No Architectural/Engineering** – Closely tied to the guidelines discussed above regarding structural work, the FHA indicates that if there is anything about the nature of the project that requires work of a licensed architect or engineer, the project must be handled as a Standard 203k.

▶ *Landscaping/Site Improvements O.K. vs. No Landscaping/Site Improvements* – To add to the flexibility of the Standard 203k, the FHA allows site and landscaping improvements. This includes a new driveway and walks, grading of the yard, exterior drainage, etc. The Streamline does not allow these kinds of improvements, with the exception of repairs to a water well or a septic system. Even though these are activities typically considered site improvements, the FHA does allow these exceptions for a Streamline K up to a limit approved by your lender.

▶ *$5,000 Minimum Repairs vs. No Minimum Repairs* – Without at least $5,000 in repair work to be done, the FHA will simply not approve a Standard 203k. The Streamline does not have this minimum, although with the additional fees and effort associated with securing a 203k loan over a normal FHA loan, most will agree that it doesn't make much sense to use a 203k for less than $5,000 of work.

▶ *203k Consultant Required vs. No Consultant Required* – A 203k Consultant, also known as a "HUD Consultant", is a professional approved by the FHA to provide specific services to the benefit of the parties involved in the 203k project. These include an inspection of the home, identifying mandatory repairs and creating a "work write-up" that details the scope of work for the project. We'll get into more detail on the role of the 203k Consultant later on, but be aware for now that the use of this consultant is mandatory on a Standard, but optional on a Streamline.

▶ *Up to Five Draws vs. 50% Upfront + Final Draw* – Just as it is in a construction loan, the term "draw" here is used to describe a payment made to the contractor against the total contract amount for the renovation work. In the case of a Standard 203k, which is typically more complicated with more moving pieces, the lender is allowed to make up to a maximum of five separate draw payments to the contractors working on the project. These are typically scheduled on a once-per-month basis.

The Streamline 203k, with its focus on more simple projects, allows a total of two draws. The first draw, however, is allowed to be made just prior to the start of the project for up to 50 percent of the contract amount. The final draw is then made at completion for the balance of the contract amount. Later on, as we go through the transaction process and work flow, we'll look at the specifics of the paperwork and how these draws are made.

▶ **Inspections for Each Draw vs. Final Inspection if More than $15,000** – This is tied to the draw schedule discussed above. For a Standard 203k, each draw request by the contractor requires a site inspection by a third-party inspector to verify the completion of work. This is the same approach used on new construction loans and is designed to make sure the contractor gets paid for only work properly completed at each draw.

Since the first draw on a Streamline is made prior to the start of work, there is no inspection required. At the completion of the project, if the total renovation work exceeded $15,000, the FHA requires a final inspection prior to disbursement of the final draw payment. This again is an area where we find the lender may become more restrictive. Even though the FHA does not require it, some lenders will choose to have a final inspection made even though the project was less than $15,000. Although there's an additional expense for this draw, these lenders feel this extra step reduces risk for everyone involved.

▶ **10% Holdback Required vs. No Holdbacks Required** – Taking the draw process a step further, to provide a level of additional insurance against the contractor getting ahead of the game in payments, the FHA requires a 10 percent holdback on each draw. A "holdback" refers to a percentage of each draw that is held back and paid along with the final payment at project completion. This is a common practice in the commercial construction industry, although it does occur in large-scale residential construction as well. As indicated, there is no holdback requirement on Streamline K's.

▶ **10% Contingency Reserve Required vs. Contingency Reserve Optional** – Sometimes confused with a holdback, a contingency reserve is an amount that is added to the renovation escrow to allow for unanticipated cost overruns. If you remember the movie Money Pit, I'm sure you'll understand the logic behind the contingency reserve!

The old adage in the world of construction is "everything takes twice as long and costs twice as much as originally anticipated." This is at least equally true in the world of remodeling. We just can't know for sure what's behind those walls, or what other surprises might come about as we dig into this project. The older the property and the more complex the renovation work, the more likely we'll encounter unanticipated challenges, which often lead to additional costs.

As a result, even though it's not required on Streamlines, you'll find most lenders mandating a minimum 10 percent contingency reserve on all 203k loans, and sometimes even 15 percent or more for very old properties or especially complicated projects. It's also common to require a minimum of 15 percent contingency when inspections and cost estimates have been made for a property where utilities have not been turned on.

▸ *Up to Six Months PITI If Not Habitable vs. Maximum 30 Days Not Habitable –* You may be familiar with the abbreviation commonly used in real estate: "PITI," which stands for "Principal, Interest, Taxes and Insurance." These are the four typical components of a mortgage payment.

The idea here is that once you take ownership of your new home, you begin to make monthly payments (PITI) on the 203k mortgage. If the home is not habitable at any point during the renovation, you could incur the expense of your new home mortgage, as well as the cost of living in an alternative residence, very likely a rental of some sort.

To help overcome this financial burden, guidelines for the Standard 203k allow you to include funds in the renovation escrow to cover this addition cost. It's allowable to include an amount equal to the monthly PITI for each month the home will not be habitable, up to a maximum of six months. Remembering the Streamline 203k is intended for less complicated projects, the FHA does not allow any funds to be included for this purpose. In fact, if it's expected the home will not be habitable for more than 30 days, the use of a Standard K is required.

▸ *More Eligible Improvements vs. Fewer Eligible Improvements –* Keeping in mind that the Standard K allows structural improvements as well as exterior site improvements, the list of eligible improvements is greater for a Standard than a Streamline. Since there's a lot of detail provided by the FHA relative to improvements that are eligible and those that are ineligible, we'll dedicate the next chapter to listing these specifics.

Chapter 8

203k Eligible, Ineligible and Required Repairs

As discussed earlier, most people are surprised at the wide variety of repairs and improvements allowed under FHA 203k guidelines. Even though the Streamline is focused on simpler, non-structural activities, it's surprising how many different things can be done to bring a home back to life and make it your own. The following provides an overview of allowable 203k improvements as described by the FHA.

What improvements are eligible under the Streamline 203k?
The Streamline 203k program is intended to facilitate uncomplicated rehabilitation and/or improvements to a home for which plans, consultants, engineers and/or architects are not required. This program allows discretionary improvements and/or repairs shown below:

▶ Repair/replacement of roofs, gutters and downspouts

▶ Repair/replacement/upgrade of existing HVAC systems

▶ Repair/replacement/upgrade of plumbing and electrical systems

▶ Repair/replacement of flooring

▶ Minor remodeling, such as kitchens, which does not involve structural repairs

▶ Painting, both exterior and interior

▶ Weatherization, including storm windows and doors, insulation, weather stripping, etc.

▶ Purchase and installation of appliances, including free-standing ranges, refrigerators, washers/dryers, dishwashers and microwave ovens

▶ Accessibility improvements for persons with disabilities

▶ Lead-based paint stabilization or abatement of lead-based paint hazards

▶ Repair/replace/add exterior decks, patios, porches

▶ Basement finishing and remodeling, which does not involve structural repairs

▶ Basement waterproofing

- Window and door replacements and exterior wall re-siding
- Septic system and/or well repair or replacement

What items are ineligible for the Streamline 203k?

Properties that require the following work items are not eligible for financing under the Streamline 203k:

- Major rehabilitation or major remodeling, such as the relocation of a load-bearing wall;
- New construction (including room additions);
- Repair of structural damage;
- Repairs requiring detailed drawings or architectural exhibits;
- Landscaping or similar site amenity improvements;
- Any repair or improvement requiring a work schedule longer than six (6) months; or
- Rehabilitation activities that require more than two (2) payments per specialized contractor.

    Mortgagors may not use the Streamline 203k program to finance any required repairs arising from the appraisal that do not appear on the list of Streamline 203k-eligible work items or that would:

- Necessitate a "consultant" to develop a "Specification of Repairs/Work Write-Up;"
- Require plans or architectural exhibits;
- Require a plan reviewer;
- Require more than six months to complete;
- Result in work not starting within 30 days after loan closing; or
- Cause the homeowner to be displaced from the property for more than 30 days during the time the rehabilitation work is being conducted. (FHA anticipates that, in a typical case, the homeowner would be able to occupy the property after mortgage loan closing).

What improvements are _required_ under the Standard 203k?

▸ Addition to existing structure. New construction must conform with local codes and HUD Minimum Property Standards.

▸ Weather strip all doors and windows to reduce infiltration of air when existing weatherstripping is inadequate or nonexistent.

▸ Caulk or seal all openings, cracks or joints in the building envelope to reduce air infiltration.

▸ Insulate all openings in exterior walls where the cavity has been exposed as a result of the rehabilitation. Insulate ceiling areas where necessary.

▸ Adequately ventilate attic and crawl space areas.

What improvements are _eligible_ under the Standard 203k?

▸ Structural alterations and reconstruction (e.g., repair or replacement of structural damage, chimney repair, additions to the structure, installation of an additional bath(s), skylights, finished attics and/or basements, repair of termite damage and the treatment against termites or other insect infestation, etc.).

▸ Changes for improved functions and modernization (e.g., remodeled bathrooms and kitchens, including permanently installed appliances, i.e., built-in range and/or oven, range hood, microwave, dishwasher).

▸ Elimination of health and safety hazards (including the resolution of defective paint surfaces or lead-based paint problems on homes built prior to 1978).

▸ Changes for aesthetic appeal and elimination of obsolescence (e.g., new exterior siding, adding a second story to the home, covered porch, stair railings, attached carport).

▸ Reconditioning or replacement of plumbing (including connecting to public water and/or sewer system), heating, air conditioning and electrical systems. Installation of new plumbing fixtures is acceptable, including interior whirlpool bathtubs.

▸ Installation of well and/or septic system. The well or septic system must be installed or repaired prior to beginning any other repairs to the property.

▸ Roofing, gutters and downspouts

▸ Flooring, tiling and carpeting

▶ Energy conservation improvements (e.g., new double pane windows, steel-insulated exterior doors, insulation, solar domestic hot water systems, caulking and weatherstripping, etc.)

▶ Major landscape work and site improvement, (e.g. patios, decks and terraces that improve the value of the property equal to the dollar amount spent on the improvements or required to preserve the property from erosion)

▶ The correction of grading and drainage problems

▶ Tree removal if the tree is a safety hazard to the property

▶ Repair of existing walks and driveway if it may affect the safety of the property

▶ Fencing, new walks and driveways, and general landscape work (i.e., trees, shrubs, seeding or sodding) cannot be in the first $5,000 requirement

▶ Improvements for accessibility to a disabled person

▶ New, free-standing range, refrigerator, washer and dryer, trash compactor, etc.

▶ Interior and exterior painting

▶ The repair of a swimming pool, not to exceed $1,500. Repair costs exceeding the $1,500 limit must be paid into the contingency reserve fund by the borrower.

What improvements are _ineligible_ under the Standard 203k?

▶ Improvements that do not become a permanent part of the real property

▶ Luxury items, such as...

▶ Barbecue pit; bathhouse; dumbwaiter; exterior hot tub; sauna, spa and whirlpool bath; outdoor fireplace or hearth; photo mural; installation of a new swimming pool; gazebo; television antenna; satellite dish; tennis court; tree surgery, etc.

▶ Additions or alterations to provide for commercial use

I think for the most part, you'll find this list provides a pretty clear overview of what's allowed and what's not. The message here again is to turn to your lender for clarification as it relates to your specific project and desired improvements.

As we talk about all of these eligible repairs and improvements, it's also important to remember that, ultimately, the total amount of money spent and the types of improvements being made are going to have to be reconciled with the completed value of the property. In other words, the appraisal will have to show that the total cost of the home purchase plus improvements is not going to exceed the anticipated finished value of the property. This is critical for loan approval. It's possible that some improvements may simply not add enough additional value relative to their cost, regardless of whether these improvements are considered eligible by the FHA. We'll explore the appraisal and related considerations as we work through the 203k transaction process in upcoming chapters.

Chapter 9

An Intimidating Process

We've already covered quite a bit of ground together as we explore our "Best Kept Secret." I'm hopeful that as you learn more, you're also getting excited about how you can benefit from the power of a renovation loan. I've talked to many folks who become very excited once they better understand this great opportunity. As you would expect, however, some people who love the idea of what a renovation loan can do for them are, at the same time, intimidated by what they feel might be a complicated process.

This intimidation is not only found in potential homebuyers or homeowners. I find this reaction also comes up regularly with real estate agents and loan officers. "A 203k deal just has too many moving parts," they'll say. "There are too many things to go wrong and too many ways we could run into delays."

Before I tell you my response to these kinds of comments, Teresa is going to share a story:

Every year, Dennis and I attend major real estate conventions, often as both speakers and exhibitors, which allows us to connect with thousands of agents and brokers. These events are not only excellent for promoting our REbuildUSA program, but also for networking and learning about what's going on in real estate throughout the U.S. and beyond.

At a recent international convention for one of the industry's largest brands, we were approached by an agent (we'll call him Bob) who was especially eager to get registered to participate in our program. He listened carefully as I explained our 203k Specialist designation training course and the other benefits of membership, but before I was finished, he said, "How do I get started? This is exactly what I need."

"You're definitely a man who knows what he wants," I laughed. "Let's get you signed up right here and you can start working on your training today if you like."

As Bob typed his information into the computer, I commented that he seemed pretty excited about getting started. "Are you currently working on a 203k deal?"

"Actually, I'm working right now with a number of buyers and I want to know this stuff right away because I need to make them all aware of the 203k and how this works."

"That's fantastic," I replied, "I wish more agents would have that same attitude."

"You're right," said Bob, "all of them should...and let me tell you, I learned that the hard way."

He then went on to explain to me that after 20 years as a top producing agent, he had recently had a very upsetting experience. A few weeks earlier, Bob had received a phone call from one of his customers who had moved in to her home several months ago. She had been very happy with his service and really loved the home, so Bob thought she may have been calling with a referral.

He was shocked to hear her very upset as she shouted into the phone, "Are you not aware of the FHA 203k Loan program?"

"Well, yes I am," Bob stammered.

"Then why didn't you tell me about it? Isn't it part of your job to make me aware of my options? Isn't that why people turn to you as a real estate professional?"

Before he could respond, she continued, "You were well aware I wanted to put in new flooring and new appliances. You knew I wanted to repaint and do some other updating. Don't you think you should have told me about the 203k?"

She went on to explain that she had invested 20 percent in the down payment, and then cashed in early on some retirement funds to pay for the improvements. If she had been aware of the 203k, she could have enjoyed a much more financially sound solution, and could have kept her retirement funds in place.

Attempting to explain himself, Bob responded, "The reason I didn't mention the 203k is because those loans often take a lot more work and can be a real hassle."

"More work for whom? A real hassle for whom? If you're talking about *me, then don't you think that's my decision to make? I hope you aren't saying that it was too much of a hassle for you to help me get the right loan!"*

Putting yourself in the shoes of that homebuyer, I'm sure you would have felt very much the same. Bob agreed with her and realized he had been acting in a way that was clearly not professional and not looking out for the best interest of his clients. Although, clearly not intentionally done, he felt terribly about having let her down.

I'm happy to say that not only did Bob very quickly complete his training, but he also made it his mission to spread the word on the benefits of the 203k to everyone who would listen. We talked again several months later as Bob was working to organize a series of 203k Consumer Seminars to help more people become aware of this powerful road to homeownership that so few understand.

Sadly, this type of situation occurs all too often when real estate agents or loan officers don't take the responsibility to be educated on all of the best options for their customers. Can you imagine a situation where a doctor compromises your health or mobility simply because he was too lazy to learn about a new procedure that was better for his patients? Can you imagine recovering from surgery and learning that an alternative treatment that actually gets better results could have been done without surgery? And can you imagine your doctor explaining that even though he knew about this alternative, he just didn't feel like dedicating the time to take the training—and instead, decided to use the old approach? I often share this scenario and ask these questions in my presentations to lenders and realtors. And I can assure you, for most, the message comes through loud and clear.

So there's clearly an important lesson here for lenders and real estate agents. There's also a valuable lesson for you. It's important for you to work with true professionals to support you in the purchase or refinance of a home. Just as you would when selecting a doctor, an attorney or other professional, make sure you check references. Find out what you can about this person's commitment to continuing education and awareness of the latest information, strategies, market conditions, etc. Make the extra effort to reach out to past clients to gain their perspectives on this agent or lender. You deserve the highest level of professional support, especially for what may be one of the most substantial investments in your life.

Taking this further, I'd like to emphasize the importance for you to not become intimidated by a process that may seem daunting. One of my goals in writing this book was not only to share the opportunities presented by renovation loans, but to also help you overcome the fear you may have about living through the process. As with so many things in life, once we have an understanding of how things work and what to realistically expect, the less intimidating it seems. To that end, the next chapters are dedicated to taking the mystery out of the details of the 203k transaction process.

Chapter 10

The 203k Transaction – Getting Started

As we get started through the steps in the transaction process, it's important for you to recognize that, as in many other endeavors, there's more than one road to follow that will ultimately get you where you'd like to go. I'll make sure to point out some of the "have-to-do's" or strict guidelines along the way, but as you work with your loan officer and real estate agent, you'll find the sequence of activities and timing can vary depending on the particulars of your specific transaction. Each deal is as unique as you are, so having some level of flexibility is a good thing!

The process we'll be discussing here is a 203k purchase transaction. We'll be contrasting the steps and details between a Standard and a Streamline as we go, but again, this process focuses on the steps relative to finding a home to purchase and renovate using a 203k loan. As we go through the next chapters, we'll talk about each of these steps in depth. Here's a brief overview of the process we're going to cover as a quick reference:

The 203k Purchase Transaction Process

1. Meet with Your Renovation Loan Officer

2. Find Your New Home

3. Develop Renovation Value Analysis

4. Offer Presented and Accepted

5. Home Inspection or HUD Consultant

6. Meet with Contractor/Scope of Work and Bids Prepared

7. Submit Final Renovation Contract Docs to Lender

8. Appraisal Ordered

9. Appraisal Completed and Loan Approval Finalized

10. Loan Is Closed and Renovation Funds Set up in Escrow

11. Renovation Work Begins

12. Project Competed

For those of you interested in refinancing using a 203k, I think you will find it pretty easy to identify those steps and details that relate to your transaction. One of the most obvious differences is the fact that you would typically not involve a real estate agent in a refinance transaction. And, of course, you're not shopping, evaluating the comparative value of potential properties, or working your way through offers and purchase agreements. At the same time, many of the concepts and requirements are identical, and getting a good appraisal to correctly establish the value of your home following renovation is important as well.

Before we move on, I'd like to share a few words of caution. As you move through the transaction process, you'll be dealing with a number of different professionals and discussing many important details. Your ability to keep track of these details and minimize confusion can make all the difference in the success of your project and the quality of your renovation loan experience. Here are few suggestions:

▸ Take carefully detailed notes of your conversations with your lender, REALTOR®, contractor, inspectors, suppliers and others involved in your project, whether over the phone or face-to-face. Include names, dates, responsibilities and next steps. You may want to confirm important details in emails to assure a clear understanding and have the benefit of a "paper trail."

▸ As much as you may hate contracts and other related documents, it's essential to actually read them and clearly understand what's in writing. It's much easier to resolve misunderstandings up-front than after a problem or dispute has come about.

▸ Never sign documents that are not completely filled in. In spite of how much you trust the professionals you're working with, errors and mistakes could appear that create serious issues later on. Tell them that you just can't sleep at night if you've signed any form of agreement or paperwork that was not a completed document and hold your ground on this one.

▸ Always insist on copies of signed documents and keep these securely stored away for later reference if necessary. Even when dealing with people with the very best intentions, having the original document as a reference can become critical to resolving a misunderstanding at any point down the line.

With this in mind, let's now get started on our journey together through a 203k Renovation Loan transaction.

Transaction Step # 1 - *Meet with Your Renovation Loan Officer*
Remembering the advice I've shared regarding the importance of your lender in guiding you through the process, your first stop on the 203k train ride is a meeting with your loan officer. Your goals here are to get a pre-approval from the lender—and remembering my rule that your lender is your quarterback, also to discuss the steps, requirements and timing as it relates to your specific situation and this lender's process.

What is a "pre-approval?" This is a term that often gets confused with "pre-qualification," so it's important for you to understand the difference.

A pre-qualification is best seen as a ballpark estimate of how much money a particular lender might be willing to lend to you. For a pre-qualification, the lender does not require actual financial documents, but instead relies on a verbal interview in-person or by phone, to get an idea of your financial picture. You provide information regarding income, debts, assets, etc. and the lender will give you a rough idea of how much home you can afford. Although this is helpful for preliminary planning purposes, it's important to have a true pre-approval in place before actually shopping for a home.

A pre-approval, although a conditional commitment, is a more accurate indication of what amount of mortgage funds this particular lender would be willing to lend you. The pre-approval, as you would expect, does require the submission of actual financial documentation. Pre-approval also typically requires an application fee, since the lender orders credit reports, verifies employment and then issues an actual commitment letter.

The pre-approval, then, gives you a more accurate idea of how much home you can afford. What's also important here is that sellers and their agents will be much more interested in working with you and accepting an offer you may choose to make on a property. At the same time, realize that this approval is conditional upon finding a specific home, entering into a purchase agreement, having firm bids in hand for your repairs and renovation work, and then securing an appraisal that supports the loan. At the pre-approval stage then, the lender is not locked in to funding a mortgage for you—and you're not locked in to enter into a mortgage agreement with this lender.

So in this first meeting with your lender, you'll work on getting the wheels turning for your pre-approval. You should also have a discussion to allow you to clearly understand the steps, timing, required documentation and other details of this lender's renovation loan process. I encourage you to take detailed notes and gather any written guidelines, forms, checklists, etc., the loan officer might have available. I also suggest you work with the loan officer and your real estate agent to lay out a sample timeline which will also help to clarify the steps in the process. Some of the areas of your discussion should include:

▶ Overview of transaction process

▶ Identify your responsibilities as a buyer

▶ Document requirements from you

▶ Contractor documents and validation requirements

▶ Home Inspection/203k Consultant requirements and timing

▶ List of all costs, including contingency reserve requirements

▶ Appraisal requirements and timing

▶ Final approval requirements

▶ Timing to closing, escrow funding

▶ Timing for draw disbursement, final draw and closeout

▶ Understanding the Good Faith Estimate

Following this meeting and securing your pre-approval, which typically comes together pretty quickly, you should be well-armed with the information you need to begin shopping for your new home.

Chapter 11

The 203k Transaction – Finding Your Home and Renovation Value Analysis

Transaction Step #2 – *Find Your New Home*
Now that you know where you stand financially, your skilled 203k Specialist real estate professional should next step in to lead the charge. An experienced agent guides you carefully through the process of finding a great home in a great location that can be renovated to best meet your budget and needs.

Just as your lender is your quarterback relative to the details, documents and requirements of the loan process, your real estate agent is your quarterback in your search for the ideal home. Your agent will identify potential properties, help you analyze value, coordinate the submission of offers, facilitate negotiations, prepare purchase agreements and other documents, and help keep the purchase process moving forward successfully.

It's important to recognize that your pre-approval identifies the total amount of home mortgage you can afford. If you were shopping for a move-in-ready home, you would be searching for a home priced at or near this pre-approval amount. In the case of a renovation loan, the pre-approval amount represents the total of the money available to fund the purchase as well as renovation work desired. For example, if you are pre-approved for a $200,000 renovation loan amount, you'll be shopping for homes you might buy for somewhere in the range of $150,000 to $180,000, with the understanding that the balance of funds be used for repairs and improvements. It's possible you might find homes priced even much less than this that offer great potential.

As you can imagine, this is where having the support of a real estate agent who has the training and understanding of the renovation loan transaction process is very important. Their knowledge of the area, specific neighborhoods and floor plans, as well as relative property values will be invaluable to you. They couple this with an understanding of your needs, tastes and priorities. Altogether, this knowledge allows them to help you find the best "diamonds in the rough" for you to renovate into your dream home.

An experienced renovation loan specialist should also have the ability to help you develop a rough "guesstimate" of the costs of repairs and improvements you're considering. As you consider improvements, your real estate professional can also help you evaluate what makes sense and what might not. They should provide guidance as you consider the impact on resale value and potential return on investment if that's of importance to you.

You may be familiar with the abbreviation "CMA," which stands for "competitive market analysis" or "comparative market analysis." This is an analysis of market data commonly used by real estate agents to compare property values. In the case of a renovation loan, we are interested in what's done in a typical CMA, but we need to take this analysis even further. For this analysis, I've coined the term *Renovation Value Analysis,* or *RVA.*

Transaction Step #3 – *Develop Renovation Value Analysis*

So what's a Renovation Value Analysis?

The idea behind the RVA is that, as a homebuyer utilizing a renovation loan, you want to make a meaningful financial analysis of the property. This analysis considers the initial purchase as well as the cost and impact of the renovation. Since most buyers are not willing to spend any more money than absolutely necessary before having an offer accepted, we're typically going to be doing this analysis before having the benefit of a home inspection or appraisal.

So, similar to what's done to develop a CMA, your real estate agent is going to mix together some market research, a little art, a little science and a dash of good, old-fashioned gut intuition to come up with some reasonable "guesstimate" numbers. For an effective RVA, I recommend you and your agent work through these four steps together:

1. *Estimate Value of the Home in Current (As-Is) Condition* – Based on any market data available, what would be your best guess of the value of this property in its current, unrepaired, unrenovated, perhaps even distressed, beat-up

condition? As is done in an appraisal, the approach here is to identify "comparables" or "comps." The question we're asking and answering is what are the values of comparable homes in comparable neighborhoods in comparable condition?

2. *Estimate Value of Home in Renovated Condition* – The next question we ask and answer is "What are the values of comparable homes in comparable locations in renovated condition?" This can be referred to as the "subject to," "completed as" or "after renovation" value. In other words, this is the value of the property subject to a number of specific improvements. So we're going to do our best to find comps that help us estimate the value of this home if it were all fixed up, modernized and improved. As you can imagine, this can be challenging since close comps can sometimes be difficult to find. Again, this is where the experience of a skilled real estate agent can be invaluable.

3. *Estimated Costs of Repair and Renovation* – The goal here is to come up with a rough idea, at the very least, for what it's going to cost to get this home renovated to meet your needs and put the home in a condition that's in conformance with applicable health and safety codes. I'm going to come back to this in just a few minutes to give you a few ideas about how to come up with some meaningful numbers.

4. *Final Value Analysis* – This is where you analyze your numbers in the first three steps. How do they add up? Is the value of the home as it sits, plus the renovations costs, less than or equal to the anticipated value after renovation? Does it make financial sense to renovate this property?

If not, it may be that your estimate of the current value of the home is too high. It's also possible that the improvements you have in mind just don't offer much of a return on the investment.

Ultimately, what you feel brings you the greatest value is a personal decision. Only you can decide what a "good investment" means to you. Here's a story I share in my real estate training that relates to this:

There was an old man who loved to go outside for a walk on nice sunny days. Right alongside his home was a footpath that runs along the edge of a small pond. One nice, sunny day, as he's very slowly walking along this path, he hears a voice and stops. He looks around for a moment, but doesn't see anyone there, and decides he must be have imagined the voice. Shrugging his shoulders, he takes just a few more steps and stops as he again hears a voice calling out to him. Turning around, the old man looks down and there on the ground right next to his feet at the edge of this path is a big old frog looking up at him smiling.

As you would expect, the old man is amazed at what he's seeing and hearing, and blurts out, "Are you kidding me...could this be a talking frog?"

The frog responds, "That's right, I'm a talking frog. But that's not all. If you pick me up and you kiss me, I'll become the most beautiful woman you've ever imagined—the woman of your dreams!"

The old man breaks into a smile as the frog continues, "But there's even more. I will also be your servant. Anything you ever desire of me, whenever you desire it, will be yours"

As you would guess, he's amazed by this and, grinning from ear to ear, picks up the frog, puts it in his pocket, and starts again to slowly mosey on down the path. He's only taken a few steps when he hears a muffled voice in his pocket. He stops walking, opens the pocket, looks in and asks the frog, "What's wrong?"

"Aren't you going to kiss me?" the frog asks.

"Are you kidding?" the old man answers, "At my age, I'd rather have a talking frog!"

I'm sure you'll agree that this story makes an important point. We all have our own perspectives on what's desirable, what makes sense, or what's of great value. We can't tell by looking at someone what's most important to them. At the same time, others can't know what's most important to us either—yet people often do make assumptions in this regard. As I share this message with salespeople in my training, I offer them a concept I call Buyer Value Perspectives to explore different ways that people might perceive the value proposition on a 203k renovation loan.

Buyer Value Perspectives

The concept here is that for different people, we can find different perspectives as to what they feel gives them the greatest value in a home purchase and renovation project. My Buyer Value Perspectives describe three different schools of thought regarding the completed value of their renovated home relative to the estimated market value of comparable homes.

1. *Equal Value Perspective* – Once they've completed the desired renovations, some buyers will be happy to find that the value of their home is more or less in line with the value of similar homes in similar renovated condition. In other words, they don't want to be upside down relative to comparable homes, but also aren't focused on gaining substantial equity in the process. We can visualize this perspective by putting it into a simple formula:

   Purchase Price + Renovation Costs is equal to the Estimated Market Value of the renovated home.

   In this case, the idea is that although no new equity has been created through the process, the homeowners feel they've made a good investment since they now have a home that's repaired and improved to reflect their tastes and needs. In effect, this gives them more home for their money, as its customized for their lifestyle at essentially no additional cost over buying a different home in move-in-ready condition.

2. *Equity Value Perspective* – What we're talking about here is that some buyers will expect that in addition to covering the renovation costs, they should also earn some amount of sweat equity in the process. They expect some amount of financial reward for taking on the renovation project, investing the time and effort for planning, coordinating contractors and other details. In other words, these are folks saying, "I think this a great idea. I should be able to get a great buy on a house, but I should also come out ahead financially in the process."

   The good news is that in a lot of market areas, we're finding opportunities for homebuyers to make this happen. The critical factors here include finding a very competitively priced home and keeping renovation costs to a more conservative level. Our formula for *Equity Value Perspective* would look like this:

Purchase Price + Renovation Costs is less than the Estimated Market Value of the renovated home

I'm sure many buyers find this perspective desirable, but it's clearly relative to their tastes in finishes, products and other improvement details as well. For those buyers who put an emphasis on the value of higher-end or custom products and finishes, I offer one more perspective:

3. *Premium Value Perspective* – These are buyers who are willing to actually pay a premium in the long run to end up with a home that better reflects their tastes and meets their needs. Instead of paying a premium price for a home in excellent condition, but in the process, also paying for colors, finishes and details chosen by the previous homeowners, the 203k renovation process will allow them to ultimately end up with a home that includes more of what they really want and need.

Here's our *Premium Value Perspective* formula:

Purchase Price + Renovation Costs is somewhat greater than the Estimated Market Value of the renovated home

These homeowners are happy to pay at least some amount of premium to have a home that really meets their needs, and whatever the combination of location, colors, finishes, design, convenience and lifestyle that appeals to them most, we know many people willing to pay a little more to get what they really want.

I hope you find these perspectives helpful as you consider what you're looking for in a home purchase or renovation refinance loan. Please also keep in mind that the financial benefits go beyond simply what's considered in the simple value formulas I offer above. As you replace older materials, appliances and systems in your home, you also minimize upcoming repair costs and utility expenses. As a result, you might find that the closer you move from the Equity Value Perspective to the Premium Value Perspective, depending on the actual improvements made, you could realize a greater financial return over the long run in additional savings.

With our Buyer Value Perspectives in mind, let's now return again to our Renovation Value Analysis.

One key component of the Renovation Value Analysis is creating a rough estimate—or "guesstimate," if you will—of the costs to make the desired repairs and improvements. As you may be aware, it's not unusual for prospective homebuyers to make a similar type of analysis in a conventional purchase transaction. However, in the case of a renovation loan, it's an essential element of the process as we evaluate affordability and determine an offering price for a home we may want to make an offer to purchase.

So what would be some of the steps in the process of coming up with this guesstimate? Let's take a look:

1. **Develop Preliminary Scope of Work** – A very important key to our success with any renovation loan is focusing enough attention on clearly identifying the scope of work. This is essential to ending up with the very best value in a home that truly meets your needs. Recognizing that we often run into budget limitations, the repairs and improvements should be organized into at least three categories of importance or priority. I suggest the following:

   a. **Must Do's** – This category includes mandatory repairs that will be required by the FHA to meet HUD Minimum Property Standards, such as safety and health issues, energy efficiency, etc. You also want to include in the "Must Do's" category those improvements you feel are essential to making this house your home. Beyond the mandatory required repairs, the balance of the items and how you categorize them is clearly up to you on a personal basis.

   b. **Should Do's** – Although these are lesser priority, the goal is to include as many of the "Should Do's" as our budget will allow. For example, it would be desirable to replace a roof that may have only a few more years of useful life. Another common example would be making improvements that would result in lower energy bills, such as higher efficiency heating and cooling equipment. Once you have a thorough home inspection done on a property, this list of "Should Do's" usually grows.

   c. **Like to Do's** – These include things like updating, redecorating or lifestyle desires. These are finishes, fixtures, features, etc., you would like to enjoy in your finished home, but not having these items is not necessarily a deal breaker.

2. *Take Photos and Rough Measurements* – While you're walking through the home, it can be very helpful to take photos that can serve as a reference as you continue your evaluation and planning. These photos should include overall rooms as well as shots of areas requiring repair or other improvements. These can be helpful to share with a contractor or with someone in a home improvement store or showroom helping you choose materials and finishes.

It's also important for someone, whether you or your real estate agent, to get to work with a tape measure. What do we want to measure? Anything that will be helpful for reference as we're shopping for finish materials, cabinetry and such. If we're thinking about replacing cabinets and countertops, it's helpful to measure the longest distance, typically where the cabinets meet the wall at the backsplash area. What we're looking for here are lineal foot measurements. For an island, we'll want to get length and width dimensions.

For flooring we simply want the floor dimensions of a room, so that's not too difficult. Those same floor dimensions, along with a rough measurement of the room height, are also going to be helpful to determine painting costs. If we're thinking about replacement windows, let's get some window dimensions and let's get a count on the number of windows. For roofing, what we'll need are outside dimensions around the home along with a few photos that will offer an idea of the pitch and complexity roof. I'm sure you'll agree this is pretty much common sense. We're trying to collect basic information that will be helpful as we're trying to come up with rough, preliminary estimates of renovation costs.

3. *Compile Rough Estimates* – At this point, there are a number of possible directions you can turn to pull together some meaningful cost estimates. Here are a few suggestions:

   a. *Technology Solutions* – Keep in mind that the world of technology is constantly bringing new solutions and resources to the table. You can find renovation cost estimating apps for your tablet and websites with calculators based on national remodeling cost databases. You can also find technology where you upload photos that are then enabled to allow you to virtually change materials, colors and finishes as a powerful virtualization tool. So I encourage you to reach out and look for any of the latest tech solutions available. I also encourage you to visit us online at REbuildUSA where you'll find options to help in this regard.

b. *Your Lender or Agent* – Ask them for any suggestions they have on how to best pull together your rough estimates. They can typically offer recommendations of people, resources or technology solutions you'll find helpful.

c. *Local Contractors* – Although some contractors will charge for job costing up front, there are others who are happy to meet with you at the site and provide some rough estimates that can be very helpful. To get more accurate estimates, you may find it worthwhile to pay a reasonable estimating fee.

d. *Home Improvement Stores and Showrooms* – An excellent starting point for most of us is to schedule a visit to the local home improvement center or other specialty showrooms for items such as flooring, cabinetry, appliances, light fixtures, plumbing products, etc. Not only can you enjoy some professional guidance on the various product and materials, but they may be able to offer you estimates for installation services as well.

e. *HUD 203k Consultants* – I'm going to be spending more time later on in the book discussing the role of a HUD 203k Consultant. Your lender will also discuss with you and may be assigning a HUD Consultant to you, depending on the nature of your project as you move further along the transaction process. At this point, be aware that HUD Consultants can also be hired at this earlier stage to conduct what's known as a "feasibility study." In this capacity, they apply their expertise in the 203k process to conduct a preliminary inspection of your property and prepare rough cost estimates for your planning purposes.

4. *Remember to Factor in Contingency Reserve and Other Costs* – In Transaction Step No. 1, I encouraged you to ask the lender for a list of all costs related to the 203k mortgage. This will typically include a "Supplemental Origination Fee" which is intended to offset some of the lender's costs of managing the 203k loan. You'll also want to make sure you're allowing for funds that are included in the renovation escrow as a contingency reserve for unanticipated expenses.

Chapter 12

The 203k Transaction – Offer and Inspection

Transaction Step #4 – *Offer Presented and Accepted*
So you've been pre-qualified, found a home you like, gathered your info, developed guesstimates for the renovation costs, and crunched everything through a Renovation Loan Analysis. If all of the lights look to be green, your real estate professional will now facilitate the process of making an offer on the home, which often involves coordinating counter offers and additional negotiations. At the point you find yourself with an offer accepted—congratulations! You've reached a very important milestone. Hopefully you'll find yourself in the position to start bringing together the pieces to close your renovation loan.

As you prepare your offer, your agent will guide you through the various terms and conditions. One important area is establishing contingencies. Contingencies are conditions that must be met before you will be obligated to complete the purchase of this property. For example, unless you're paying cash for your home, you'll typically make the purchase of a home contingent upon securing a firm renovation loan commitment at a competitive rate to provide you the funds to purchase and renovate this home. Many purchasers will make the offer contingent upon the results of an appraisal, a home inspection or termite report. Other contingencies might include a septic inspection, a property survey or other conditions that will confirm the home is habitable and in conformance with zoning laws or other requirements.

These contingencies offer you the opportunity to rescind your offer under specific guidelines. If a home inspection, for example, uncovers additional costly repairs that will be necessary, you might choose to cancel the purchase agreement. Optionally, you could present this information to the seller, indicating your interest in completing the sale, but only if the seller were to cover the cost of these repairs. Again, this is an area where you should be able to rely on your real estate agent to provide the guidance you need.

Transaction Step #5 – *Home Inspection or HUD 203k Consultant*

In any home purchase transaction, a good real estate agent is going to recommend you hire a licensed home inspector. This is a professional who will visit the property and conduct a thorough inspection of the home. While almost everyone will agree this is important even on homes that appear to be in well maintained condition, I'm sure you'll recognize this can be even more important in an older home that requires repair and renovation. In the case of a 203k loan, what's also essential is that the home is inspected to determine what needs to be done to meet the HUD Minimum Property Standards.

If we were buying a home using a normal FHA-guaranteed purchase mortgage, it's required that the home meet the HUD Minimum Property Standards. In the case of a 203k, we need to identify what repairs will be necessary for the completed, renovated home to meet these standards. Your lender is responsible to confirm that any required repairs identified are included in the renovation scope of work.

The HUD Minimum Property Standards are designed to eliminate safety hazards and health hazards, and to assure the home meets certain minimum energy efficiency standards as well. If you'd like to learn more about the details of the HUD Minimum Property Standards, you can visit hud.gov and search the Code of Federal Regulations for "24 CFR 200.926." It's not the most exciting reading for everyone, but if you're a fan of construction details, you may have a wonderful time there. In any event, your home inspector should be familiar with these requirements and provide you a list of specific repairs required to meet these standards.

In addition, we also want the inspector to identify any other recommended repairs. These would include problems that might rear their ugly heads further down the road. This is one of the most powerful benefits of the 203k—the idea that we can anticipate these kinds of problems that might be coming down the line, get them repaired right up front, and finance them into the mortgage at a low interest rate. I think you'll agree it makes good financial sense.

Something important to know regarding the home inspection is that there is no requirement by the FHA to hire an inspector of any sort for a Streamline 203k. Many folks are surprised to learn this. For a Standard K, on the other hand, it's mandatory to hire the services of a HUD-approved 203k Consultant. The HUD Consultant will make an inspection of the home, identify the repairs necessary to meet the HUD Minimum Property Standards, and generate a "Work Write-Up," listing all required and desired repairs and improvements. The HUD Consultant will also provide estimated costs for these improvements and copies of the work write-up for your use in securing contractor bids. I'll dig deeper into the role of the HUD Consultant in a future chapter.

For all 203k's, an FHA-approved appraiser visits the property and reviews the work write-up and contractor bid documents. If the appraiser determines that all repairs necessary to meet HUD Minimum Property Standards are not included in these documents, the bids will have to be redone. This can cause significant delays, which can lead to problems as you're working to meet closing deadlines.

So I think you'll agree that although there is no FHA requirement for a home inspection on a Streamline 203k, it is highly advisable for the reasons discussed. Alternately, you could hire a HUD 203k Consultant to conduct the inspection and provide a list of property repairs and improvements in the form of a 203k work write-up. Either way, having a thorough inspection helps minimize potential surprises, delays and additional expenses down the road.

As you're considering your strategy in hiring an inspector or consultant, keep in mind it's not unusual for a project that initially appears to be a Streamline 203k and starts down that path, to change over to a Standard 203k. If the cost of renovation grows too high, or if any structural defects are discovered, the project will have to move forward as a Standard K. At this point, if you've hired a normal home inspector, you'll then have to start over again hiring a HUD Consultant. However, if you choose a HUD Consultant at the beginning, you'll be covered if the project should evolve into a Standard. For this reason, many lenders encourage the use of HUD 203k Consultants who are also licensed home inspectors. This is worth some discussion with your loan officer, since the FHA mandates that the choice of HUD Consultant is up to the lender.

Some additional advice relative to the home inspection is to **make sure utilities are turned on**. You can tell this is really important because I put it in bold letters! As you would expect, a thorough home inspection can only be done if utilities are on to make sure electrical, plumbing and HVAC issues don't go unnoticed. If your utilities are not on during inspection, some lenders may even require a higher contingency amount be included in the renovation escrow account.

I also highly recommend, if at all possible, that you and your agent meet the inspector when he or she visits the property. Many times the opportunity to ask questions and get answers right there as you're walking through the home can prove to be invaluable.

Chapter 13

The 203k Transaction – Bids and Appraisal

Transaction Step #6 – *Meet With Contractor/Scope of Work and Bids Prepared*

Now that we have either a home inspection report or our 203k Consultant work write-up, it's time to get together at the home with our contractors to finalize our scope of work for the project, discuss costs, and ultimately end up with final written bids and contract documents required by our lender. Some points to keep in mind:

▶ **Time is of the Essence** – It's important to keep things moving as quickly as possible at this stage. In the case of a home purchase, we're often working against the clock to get inspections done and other contingency items in order. For a renovation loan, it's critical to have our scope of work clearly finalized along with pricing and a contract in place with your contractor. These documents must be in your lender's hands for the scheduling of the appraisal, which is required to process your final loan approval. For these reasons, it's important to finalize decisions and material selections as quickly as possible.

▶ **Clearly Detailed Scope of Work** – I can't emphasize enough how important it is to have a clearly written, carefully itemized scope of work that supports the contract documents. We should identify colors, finishes, brand names and model numbers. Sizes and dimensions should be specified. It should also be clearly indicated that both materials and labor are included for each category or each activity.

As you are reviewing the final bids, I also recommend that you ask the contractor another key question: "What's not included?" In other words, what might be missing that could result in additional costs or delays as the project is underway?

▶ **Make Your Final Renovation Value Analysis** – Once you have final cost estimates in hand, it's time to make a final analysis of the overall investment and relative value of the completed project. Remember our earlier discussions regarding your value perspective and reconcile this with the investment you are both willing and able to make. This, again, is where your loan officer and real estate agent can be valuable resources for you. Tap into their expertise as it relates to what improvements might offer the best return on your investment. If you have any questions regarding what's allowable by the FHA, your loan officer can provide assistance. Both may be helpful when it comes to determining what improvements may be valued during the appraisal, which is an important key to final loan approval.

If you are finding that the cost of the improvement you feel neces-sary along with the purchase cost of the property come to a total that is beyond an acceptable value, you are faced with two options. One pos-sibility, especially if numbers are too far off, is to simply move on. On the other hand, there may also be an option for your agent to go back to the sellers, now armed with actual renovation bids and details, and renegotiate the purchase price. As you would imagine, these negotia-tions are sometimes successful, while in other cases, buyers will refuse to accept anything less. The good news is that more often than not, the original purchase price leaves enough room for the overall investment to add up nicely.

Transaction Step #7 – *Submit Final Renovation Contract Docs to Lender*
Your loan officer will provide a list of the documents you'll need to move forward with the final loan approval. This will include not only typical FHA loan docs, but also a signed contract with your contrac-tor, along with the detailed scope of work and relative costs. There are also additional documents required by the FHA specific to the 203k program. For example, the lender must also collect documents from your contractor to process what's called a "contractor validation." This is where the lender does some due diligence to determine the track record of the contractor as well as confirm proper licensing and insur-ance. Again, your loan officer will provide details on the contractor validation requirements.

Transaction Step #8 – *Appraisal Ordered*
Once these documents are properly completed and in hand, your lender will then order an appraisal. As you would expect, the appraisal for a renovation loan is a little different than a conventional appraisal

since the FHA is looking for the completed value of the property. As mentioned earlier, what's required here is a "completed as," "subject to" or "after renovation" appraisal. What these terms mean is that the appraiser will inspect the property and review the repairs and improvements itemized in your contractor bids. The final appraisal, then, reflects the value of the property as it will be once the renovation work is completed—or as it's sometimes said, the value of the property "subject to" the completion of these specific improvements.

If you're familiar with the appraisal that's done for a new construction loan, you'll find this is quite similar. This appraisal, by the way, must be done by an FHA appraiser specifically approved for 203k appraisals. Your lender will have qualified appraisers available to make this happen quickly.

Another unique feature of the 203k mortgage is that the FHA allows the lender to use 110 percent of the "completed as" appraisal for the maximum loan amount, minus the down payment required. This provides an additional margin that can really make a difference for many buyers. As is the case with other FHA guidelines, the lender can choose to be more restrictive, so not all lenders will allow the 110 percent appraisal. Please confirm this with your lender if you feel this will be important to you.

Transaction Step #9 – *Appraisal Completed and Loan Approval Finalized*

Our lender now receives the appraisal, and given all the numbers are adding up properly, the final loan approval is processed and a closing date is set. Congratulations! You've reached another major milestone in your journey to homeownership.

At this point, there will be additional documents to finalize, depending on what has been collected by your lender thus far. At this stage, you'll also find it beneficial to notify your contractor of the good news, as well as the anticipated closing date. This will allow the contractor to make any plans necessary to be ready to move forward as soon as the closing is successfully completed.

Chapter 14

The 203k Transaction – Closing and Renovation

Transaction Step #10 – *Loan is Closed and Renovation Funds Set Up in Escrow*

The next wild card here is how soon those funds are available to be set up in escrow. If this is a 203k Streamline, we're also hoping the first 50 percent draw payment can be quickly processed, since most contractors will be expecting this prior to the start of the renovation work.

According to the FHA, the construction must start within 30 days or less following the loan closing. And although most homeowners are eager to get things going as soon as possible, delays in setting up the renovation escrow can keep things at a standstill.

Some contractors may be willing to move forward without the initial deposit, but in many cases they will not begin your project until the funds are placed in the renovation escrow. If we're working with a Standard 203k, it's important to remember that the first draw is typically not processed until 30 days after the start of construction, so the contractor should be aware of this and prepared to handle the cash flow requirements necessary. Again, this is another example of looking to your lender for guidance on how the timing and how these details will be best handled for your project.

Transaction Step #11 – *Renovation Work Begins*

So here's one of the most exciting points in your transaction. Like most folks, you'll probably be very excited when the renovation work begins. Of course the time frame here can vary dramatically, depending on the nature of your particular project. It's not unusual to find some projects completed in a matter of three or four weeks. At the other extreme, we find complex projects involving major structural work, multiple inspections and numerous contractors coming and going before we're through. What's important to recognize is that all renovation work is required by the FHA to be completed in six months or less. This becomes an important consideration where someone might be planning a very large-scale, complicated project. You and your lender should be very careful to confirm your contractor's ability to make this happen. I highly encourage that a commitment by the contractor to meeting this requirement be included in your contract, with penalties for any additional expenses that come about as a result of non-performance.

During the renovation process, your contractor will periodically submit a draw request. Once the request is received, your lender will schedule an inspection of the property to confirm completion of the work. This will be compared against what's included in the draw request and reconciled against the cost breakdown found in the original work write-up documents. The FHA mandates a maximum of five draws for any given 203k Standard project, typically processed every thirty days. For 203k Streamlines, there are only two draws: the initial 50 percent draw, and then the final draw at completion for the balance.

Transaction Step #12 – *Project Completed*

Time for our final celebration has almost arrived as the renovation work is completed. The contractor submits a final draw request, initiating a final inspection. Then, in addition to the sign-off by the inspector, your lender will ask you to sign an acceptance letter, indicating that the project is completed to your satisfaction and in conformance with the originally contracted scope of work.

Your lender will also collect lien waivers and will disburse final payment to the contractor. You are now the proud owner of a beautiful home that has been repaired, updated and improved to your personal specifications. It's a happy day…let the games begin!

So that's our look at the key steps in a 203k transaction from start to finish. I hope you now have a much better sense of the flow of activities. I also hope you'll find this helpful as you prepare to undertake a 203k renovation loan project of your own.

Remember that each situation brings its own unique conditions, challenges and timing. As a result, I'm sure you recognize why I continue to emphasize that working with a loan officer and real estate professional who truly are 203k specialists is a very important key to your success. They'll help you navigate your way to an investment that can pay tremendous dividends, both financially and in the quality of your life.

Principle 1

The only way to get the best of an argument is to avoid it.

Chapter 15

HUD 203k Consultants

As we discussed the 203k transaction process, you'll remember I introduced the concept of the HUD 203k Consultant, often referred to as simply the "HUD Consultant." This role, initially established by the FHA in 1994, was intended to offer the option for homeowners to work with someone who would assist them in the evaluation of the property, determining the required improvements and then generating a "work write-up," or scope of work, for the project. The HUD Consultant would include both required and desired improvements and estimate approximate costs for the project. The consultant could also work as a liaison between the homeowners and the contractor to help facilitate the completion of the project. At this time, the FHA began building a roster of approved consultants organized by geographic location.

To become approved to work as a HUD Consultant, the FHA mandates the following:

To apply for placement on the FHA 203(k) Consultant Roster, an applicant must submit the information listed below to the HOC (HUD Home Ownership Center) in the area in which he/she will be conducting business. Please see HUD Mortgagee Letter 2000-25 for more information.

The application information should be submitted in the following format—a list or résumé documenting:

- A minimum of three years experience as a remodeling contractor, general contractor or home inspector. A state license as a state certified engineer or architect may be submitted in lieu of the documentation of the three years experience;

- Education;

- Licensing (general contractor, home inspector, etc.). In those states where a home inspector is required to be licensed, the Department requires the applicant to be licensed and to provide proof of that licensing;

▶ A narrative description of the current/prospective consultant's ability to per-form home inspections, prepare architectural drawings, use proper methods of cost estimating and complete draw inspections;

▶ The applicant must also submit a certification verifying that the consultant has read and fully understands the requirements of HUD Handbook 4240.4, REV 2 (203(k) Handbook) and all related materials listed in Mortgagee Letter 2000-25.

So as you can see, the HUD Consultant brings the skills of a home inspector and a contractor, with a specialized knowledge of 203k requirements, details and process. A few key points to keep in mind:

▶ *A 203k Consultant Is Required on the Standard 203k* – In the year 2000, the FHA took the role of the consultant further, making it mandatory for a HUD Consultant to be used on Standard 203k projects. This requirement does not apply to Streamline 203k's, however, some loan officers encourage their cus-tomers to use the services of a consultant on Streamlines as well.

▶ *The 203k Consultant Is Selected by the Lender* – Although it had originally been left up to the borrower to select the HUD consultant, the FHA released a mortgagee letter in July 2000, indicating that it was now the responsibility of the lender to select the 203k Consultant. The concept was to allow the lender to exercise more control over assuring the consultant provided the proper ser-vices and paperwork to minimize problems.

So what exactly are the services provided by the 203k Consultant? Here's an overview:

▶ *Feasibility Study* – Prior to making an offer on a home, a buyer may want to hire a consultant to do a quick home inspection and scope of work write-up, and run a simple financial analysis of renovating this property. This information would then help them make a better decision relative to an offering price—or maybe determine that it's not even worth moving forward on this particular property at all.

▶ *Property Inspection* – The first step for the HUD 203k Consultant is a property inspection. Although some consultants are also licensed home inspectors and provide those services as well, the focus here is first identifying the repairs that must be made to meet the HUD Minimum Code Standards. At the same time, the consultant will also review other desired improvements with the homeowner and gather necessary information to detail these improvements in the final work write-up.

▶ *Work Write-Up* – The final work write-up identifies in detail the complete scope of work. This includes the mandatory repairs required by the FHA to meet HUD Minimum Code Standards, as well as the other improvements you added from your own list. Each work item will also be shown with an estimated cost, typically calculated using software that ties to a database of localized remodeling and construction costs. This cost breakdown helps you evaluate how your desired improvements relate to your anticipated renovation budget. At this point, it's often advisable to review your wish list of desired improvements, do some additional prioritizing and make adjustments to your scope of work to stay within your budget.

Once you're satisfied with what's included in the scope of work, the work write-up can then be provided to contractors to be used as a template for the development of their bids. Keep in mind that the estimated costs provided by your HUD Consultant typically vary from the bids actually received from the contractor. Following your review of the actual bids, it's likely you'll again be prioritizing and making adjustments to the scope of work for your project.

▶ *Draw Inspections* – The lender will often hire the HUD Consultant to provide the additional service of making site inspections prior to the payment of each draw request. The Consultant will inspect the amount of work completed, reconcile the completed work to the contract bids, and approve the release of funds from the renovation escrow to be paid to the contractor.

How much do these services cost? The good news is that the FHA has established a schedule of allowable fees to be charged by HUD Consultants. You'll see by reviewing the following chart that these fees are adjusted relative to the total amount of renovation costs. Some consultants will charge additional fees for other miscellaneous services, or make adjustments if they've previously done a feasibility study on a property and are then hired to do the actual work write-up. My recommendation here is to make certain you have a clear understanding, up front and in writing, of exactly what services are being provided and at what cost. I also encourage you to review these costs with your loan officer if you have any questions or concerns.

203k Consultant Fees	
Renovation Amount	**Consulting Fee**
Up to $7,500	$400
$7,501 - $15,000	$500
$15,001 - $30,000	$600
$30,001 - $50,000	$700
$50,001 - $75,000	$800
$75,001 - $100,000	$900
More than $100,000	$1,000
Other Fees	
Feasibility Study	$100 - $200
Draw Inspection	$50 - $150

Chapter 16

The FHA Energy Efficient Mortgage

Now I'd like to introduce you to another very cool financing option called the FHA Energy Efficient Mortgage or "EEM." In a nutshell, the energy efficient mortgage is an additional amount of funds that can be added to the base mortgage for the purpose of paying for eligible energy efficient improvements. What we'll do here is go into some detail to give you a thorough understanding of this additional financial tool.

Before we dig in, I feel it's important to mention that this loan product has been around for quite some time, but like the FHA 203k, has seen very little use. In fact, there's much less awareness and much less use than the 203k. Why? Again, almost no consumers and almost no one in the real estate business have been aware that this product exists at all. Further, very few lenders have offered this product, making it all but impossible even for those who do have the awareness and desire to utilize this option. It's my hope that as we create greater awareness over time, a growing demand for the EEM will encourage more lenders to add it to the loan products on their shelves.

With this in mind, let's review some of the specifics of the EEM:

- *EEM Is Added to the Base Mortgage* – The Energy Efficient Mortgage is an FHA loan product that can be added to another base FHA mortgage. Because a 203k is already set up to handle renovation activities and features a renovation escrow account to manage these funds, it's really the ideal mortgage to take advantage of an EEM.

- *100% of EEM Costs Are Financed* – The fundamental concept here is that eligible energy efficient improvements will reduce energy costs enough to actually pay for themselves. For this reason, and the desire to improve the energy efficiency of homes across America, the FHA allows 100 percent of these energy efficient improvement costs to be financed.

- *EEM Costs Are Added to Appraised Value* – For loan purposes, 100 percent of the EEM costs are simply added to the appraised value of the home as it sits before the energy efficient mortgage. In the case of the 203k, the total cost of eligible EEM improvements is added to the "subject to" or "completed as" value of the property. In other words, you have the ability to finance these additional EEM costs even if the total mortgage exceeds the appraised value, as long as this excess amount is equal to or less than the energy efficient costs.

▶ *Total Can Exceed FHA Loan Limits* – Just as we can exceed the appraised amount, even if the base mortgage is already reaching the allowable FHA Loan Limit for the area, the EEM costs can be added on top of this.

▶ *Improvements Can Exceed $35,000 Streamline Limit* – Although a Streamline 203k has a limit of $35,000 in total renovation funds built into the mortgage, the cost of EEM improvements can be added over and above this limit while still remaining a Streamline K.

▶ *Stretch Debt-to-Income Qualifying Ratios* – Since the mortgage qualification is based on the buyer's income relative to the base amount of the loan, adding the EEM mortgage above this in effect allows us to stretch the debt-to-income ratios further than would be allowed otherwise. Again, with an understanding that these improvements pay for themselves through energy savings, higher monthly payments are offset by lower monthly utility costs.

▶ *Buyers Qualify for a Larger Loan Amount* – Another way to look at the stretching of debt-to-income ratios is that we can allow a given buyer to actually qualify for a larger mortgage with an EEM. In a case where some of the desired 203k improvements qualify for an EEM, this approach can allow them to purchase more home than they might have qualified for otherwise.

▶ *Eligible Energy Efficiency Improvements* – The improvements that qualify for use with an EEM are those that are deemed "cost-effective" energy improvements. The FHA defines these as improvements that will pay for themselves in energy savings over the expected life of the improvement made. For example, if a new HVAC system is expected to have a usable life of 20 years, this installation will qualify if the new equipment pays for itself in energy savings over this projected 20-year life span. The calculations are made at today's energy costs and estimated based on the rated efficiency of the equipment. Of course, this same type of calculation is done for any of the anticipated energy efficient improvements, whether insulation, new doors and windows, appliances, etc.

▶ *Requires HERS Rater Energy Analysis* – So who does these calculations? The FHA requires an energy audit of the home by an approved "HERS Rater." HERS stands for "Home Energy Rating System." HERS Raters are professionals, typically with experience in home inspection or construction, who undergo training and certification through certified providers who are part of the RESNET (Residential Energy Services Network) network. RESNET was founded in 1995 and operates as a non-profit organization dedicated to supporting the home energy rating industry. From the RESNET website:

RESNET's standards are officially recognized by the federal government for verification of building energy performance for such programs as federal tax incentives, the Environmental Protection Agency's ENERGY STAR program and the U.S. Department of Energy's Building America Program. RESNET standards are also recognized by the U.S. mortgage industry for capitalizing a building's energy performance in the mortgage loan, and certification of "White Tags" for private financial investors.

The RESNET website is a one-stop solution where homeowners can learn about the energy audit and rating processes, and search the RESNET directory to find certified energy auditors and raters and qualified contractors and builders. To be included in the directory, these independent, unbiased professionals must complete the required energy training to meet the high standards of excellence that RESNET demands. All RESNET-certified and RESNET-qualified professionals agree to abide by the RESNET Code of Conduct.

So what exactly does the HERS Rater do when we desire an Energy Efficient Mortgage? The HERS Rater visits the home, and using special software and approved techniques, conducts an energy audit to determine the efficiency rating of the house based on something known as the HERS Index, shown on the following page.

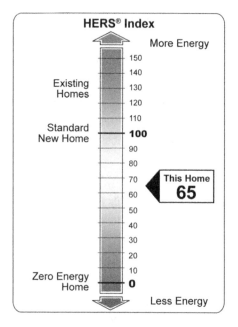

HERS Index graphic courtesy of RESNET.

If you study the index, you'll see that the higher the rating, the less efficient the home is, and the more energy it uses. Conversely, the lower the rating, the more energy efficient the home is. All the way down at the bottom of the HERS Index, we see the term "zero energy home." As you might guess, this describes a home that has been designed and constructed using the most extreme green building techniques. These homes typically incorporate some sort of passive and/or active energy generation design features as well, such as solar panels. A Zero Energy Home produces at least as much energy as it consumes in a year, achieving net zero energy consumption.

The HERS Rater visits the home and conducts an energy audit or energy analysis, gathers site data, and then crunches numbers to produce a report providing the following:

▶ The overall HERS Index rating of the house as it sits in its current condition.

▶ Recommended cost-effective energy upgrades. You can think of this as a prescription for cost-effective improvements. These might include replacing windows, higher efficiency appliances, improved insulation and weather stripping, new HVAC equipment, or similar.

▸ For each recommended improvement, an estimate of the cost, estimated annual savings, and projected useful life of the upgrades.

▸ Finally, the rater projects the HERS Index Rating for the home after the installation of recommended upgrades, with a comparison of the total annual energy savings before and after installation of the recommended upgrades.

I'm sure you can see that having this information in hand allows us to make a much better evaluation of the benefits of energy efficient improvements. It makes good sense to make improvements that pay for themselves in energy savings—and the EEM is designed to provide the funds to make that happen.

Of course, as in our 203k, there are loan limits. And the amount borrowed is subject to the appraisal and the borrower's financial capabilities. The great news is that, in many cases, the EEM allows us to obtain additional renovation funds beyond what we would have qualified for without it.

Again, keep in mind that different lenders have different guidelines and limits they sometimes establish themselves beyond the FHA requirements. Also remember that historically, not many lenders have offered EEM mortgages at all, so you may simply find this option is not available in your area.

Chapter 17

A Look at the Numbers

Looking back on what we've covered, I hope you now have a much deeper understanding of the great opportunities available through the use of a renovation loan. I think you also have a greater awareness of the process and some of the key strategies for success. At this point, I'd like to spend a few minutes reviewing an example of how the numbers add up to illustrate a renovation loan from another perspective. I know a lot of people aren't big fans of math, but for those of you who love playing around with numbers, here's your moment in the sun.

What I've done below is prepare a simple example of how the dollars and cents break down for a typical 203k Streamline loan. Keep in mind this is simply intended to provide an overview. The breakdown calculated by the lender using the Maximum Mortgage Worksheet will be more detailed.

Example 1 – Streamline 203k	
Purchase Price ("As-Is" Appraisal Value)	**$250,000**
Renovation Material and Labor Costs (detailed bids in hand)	**$32,000**
Other Allowable Costs (permits, inspections, etc.)	**$2,000**
Supplemental Origination Fee (1.5% or $350)	**$510**
Total Renovation Costs	**$34,510**
Total Purchase and Renovation	**$284,510**
"After-Improved" Appraisal Value ("subject-to" renovation)	**$300,000**
Lesser of: "After-Improved" Appraisal Value x 110% Or "As-Is" Appraisal Value + Renovation Costs	**$284,510**
Maximum Loan Amount (96.5% of above)	**$274,552**

Studying the table above, on the first row, you'll see the purchase price for the home is $250,000 in this example. In most cases, the number used here will be the actual purchase price, although if the appraised value was less, it would then be used instead. If the purchase price were greater than the as-is appraisal value of the home prior to renovation, we'd be already starting in an "upside down" situation, making it difficult for us to justify the completed cost.

The second row shows a figure of $32,000 for the total renovation funds required to make the desired improvements. To secure a loan approval, this number is based on actual written bids in hand from a validated contractor.

Our next row reflects other allowable cost categories, followed by the lender's Supplemental Origination Fee, which is an amount designed to cover some of the lender's additional administrative costs associated with a renovation loan. The FHA allows the lender to calculate this fee by multiplying the renovation costs by 1.5 percent, and using this total or $350, whichever is greater. In our example here, this calculation equals $510.

We next add these two rows together to reach a total renovation cost of $34,510—and then add this to the purchase price to reach a total purchase + renovation cost of $284,510. So you can see this figure represents the actual dollars it will take to make this project happen.

The next line here shows the "after-improved" or "subject-to" appraisal value. You'll remember this was determined by the appraiser using the scope of work and numbers found in the final bid documents from the contractor. In this example, we show an after-improved appraisal value of $300,000—so in this case the $300,000 is greater than the total cost of purchase and renovation, so that's good news. It's not unusual for the appraiser to come up with an after-improved value that's equal to the total purchase price plus renovation costs, but there are also many cases similar to this where the expected finished value is greater than the sum of the parts. That's where the sweat equity comes about.

With this information now in hand, our next step is to determine which is less—the total of actual costs or the "after-improved" appraisal value x 110%. In our example, this would total $330,000, so our lender will have to use the $284,510 since it's the lesser of these two numbers.

If, on the other hand, our total purchase and renovation costs add up to a total greater than the after-improved appraised value, we can run into a problem. What are our options? Here are some possibilities:

▸ Remember that the FHA allows the lender to add 10 percent to the after-improved appraisal value for calculating the maximum mortgage amount. If our appraisal number here was $275,000, for example, the lender could add $27,500 to this, giving us a maximum mortgage amount of $302,500. So you can see this adjustment would allow the loan to move forward.

▸ As an alternative, we might go back to the drawing board with our contractor and revise our scope of work. By reducing the cost of materials and labor, or both, we might reduce our overall renovation costs without also significantly reducing the final appraised value.

▸ Another option would be to return to the negotiation table with the sellers of the property, explaining that the costs of purchase and renovation just don't add up in line with the completed value. So even though we initially hoped our offered price was reasonable, based on this new information, we realize we can't move forward at this purchase price. At this point, your sellers might agree to lower their price—or they may hold their ground and you'll decide to move on. This is why it's important to have a reasonable contingency period to allow time to bring these numbers together. And again, this is where the guidance of a great real estate agent and a qualified loan officer becomes essential as well.

So there you have an example of some real world numbers. I hope this is helpful in bringing the various steps together from a financial perspective, and I hope this added a little extra fun if you enjoy crunching numbers.

Chapter 18

Planning and Design Advice

Now that we've covered the nuts and bolts of the 203k, we've run through the transaction process and you understand how all the pieces add up financially, I think it's time we explore some other helpful perspectives as you prepare and experience the renovation process yourself.

As you consider the realities of successfully moving through the transaction process, I'm sure it's clear that time is of the essence. Once we have an offer in place, we've got to move quickly. And this can be challenging because you may be tackling this without necessarily having much experience in the areas of remodeling or interior design.

With this in mind, I'd like to offer some advice to help you through the planning and design process.

1. **Don't be an innovator.** I think our world currently has no shortage of wild, crazy and over-the-top architecture and other design ideas. I understand you may want to make an amazing new contribution to the world of residential design, but most of us are better off not trying to be too creative. Having designed many custom homes and remodeling projects in my time, I know how many folks want to do something different and unique. And I've seen what happens when people describe their new renovation by telling their friends, "You've never seen anything like this." The end result is usually something you've never seen before—and hope you'll never see again!

My advice is: Don't reinvent the wheel. Too often people find out that what seemed like a great idea on paper, doesn't translate very well to the real world. They often end up with something they don't like, and have spent all their renovation funds making it happen. It's then too costly to change, so they live with something they don't like for a very long time.

So we don't need to take on the risk and uncertainty. There are lots of convenient places to turn where we can collect great design and decorating ideas. We can go online to any number of different websites, or visit model homes or design centers, and find all kinds of different color combinations, cabinets, products, finishes, room styles and other design details. So put on your researcher hat and find something you'd like to use as the basis for your decision making.

2. *Think about the impact on your lifestyle.* The message here is to realize that more important than the aesthetics of what we design is the fact that you're creating an environment you need to live in. So it has to be practical. It has to be right for you and your family day in and day out. As you're designing traffic areas, kitchens and baths or other spaces, really sit down and consider how you live. Where does the family gather? Are there quiet spaces, private spaces, or places to work effectively? Do you have this home designed in such a way to realistically function the way you live today, and have you thought ahead to how you might want to live differently in the future as well?

3. *Lay out spaces and furniture in advance.* It's not that difficult to go into a house with a notepad, tape measure and a camera, mark down some room dimensions and take some photos as a reference. It's also a good idea to measure door and window locations and other details that might impact furniture layout or changes you're considering. The goal then is to transfer this information to paper or maybe some of the easy-to-use design software available today. There are even apps that allow you to take photos and plug in key dimensions to create a simple floor plan. If you're challenged by technology, find someone else to help out. I always suggest that if you're having trouble with software, the internet or other technology, just find the nearest 5- or 6-year-old. They'll help you figure it out since these little ones seem to have no fear of tackling almost anything with a microprocessor or a touch screen.

Another very simple alternative is to take measurements of some of your most important pieces of furniture at home, bring that along on a pad of paper with a tape measure and then go through the house room by room to see how things will fit. Doing something this simple can help you make much better decisions.

4. *A picture paints a thousand words.* As obvious as this is, I can't tell you how many times I've had clients trying to describe something to me that they saw once before—waving their hands in the air and scribbling on a piece of paper— and still I have no idea what they're trying to tell me. Sometimes there aren't enough words to get the idea across. So the point here is to get in the habit of carrying a camera, or using the camera on your phone to capture colors, de-

signs and other ideas. Once you're in the midst of a project like this, you tend to notice these details everywhere you go. Yet, in the moment, many people just don't think to snap a photo. Make sure you do.

5. *Get organized—keep detailed notes and files.* The idea is to write stuff down when you're out shopping. Write down brand names and model numbers. Make a note of the color or take a photo and make a note of that. When you're talking with the contractor and he's sharing specific information, take notes. Keep this information organized in a file and remember again that a picture is worth a thousand words. Tear pictures out of magazines, print photos and other information you find online and keep all these things together where you can find it when you need it. Or you might take advantage of some excellent note-taking technology you can use with your computer or tablet, such as Microsoft OneNote, Evernote or similar apps.

6. *Make the commitment to make your project happen.* Planning for renovation is hard work. Be aware of that up front. Recognize that this is going to take time, energy and focus, and that you'll have to pull this all together very quickly in most situations. If this is a refinance project, you can usually do your planning at a more leisurely pace, but in a purchase situation, the clock is ticking from the moment your offer is accepted. In either case, this project only moves forward if you do what it takes to make it happen. It takes persistence and dedication. You may have to give up your bowling or poker night for a while. You may not be able to sit around watching football games for a few weeks, but unless you make the commitment and invest the necessary time, your new home dream will simply not come true.

Chapter 19

Your Renovation Survival Guide

At this point in our journey through the world of renovation loans, I'm going to switch gears again and move us ahead to one of the most important phases of our adventure. We're going to take a deep dive into the actual renovation experience. And while this is certainly an exciting time, it can also be a time that brings some real challenges. Have you seen the movie "The Money Pit?" That might give you an idea of where your renovation adventure can go if we jump in unprepared. To this point, what follows is your "Renovation Survival Guide" based on my lifetime of living in the trenches of residential construction and remodeling.

Now, for the most part, the horror stories we hear, the terrible experiences that people go through and barely survive, are due in large part to unrealistic expectations and poor communications between them and their contractors. Of course, working with poor-quality contractors is also one of the most common causes of frustration, delays and other problems.

For our purposes, we're going to assume that the education you gained from reading this book helped you through the process of choosing a qualified contractor. We'll also assume that since you were sure to be working with an experienced and knowledgeable renovation lender, your contractor was properly validated and all contracts, bid documents and other necessary paperwork is in order.

With this in mind, my goal here is to make you aware of the realities of living through the construction process, to help set you up with realistic expectations and some clear strategies to not only survive, but make your renovation experience and the end results much better.

Believe me, if anyone knows what it's like to live through construction, it's me. I literally grew up in a construction site. When I was just a baby and my eyes first began to focus, I was surrounded by construction. I was living in a home my parents were building with their own hands. Having been given an acre of land cut from my grandfather's farm, my mother and father purchased a Lincoln panelized home kit which was popular back in the '50s and '60s. After the shell was completed, my father, a skilled electrician and all around tradesman, installed wiring, insulation, sheetrock, flooring and more. My mother was his apprentice and spent many days installing flooring, wallpapering and painting while my father was at work. As soon as the basic home was reasonably finished, they began building a large family room and garage addition, so construction was always a part of my childhood memories.

My grandfather also built several homes when I was a boy, so my summers were filled with learning how to build homes from the ground up. I installed flooring, sheetrock, wiring, roofing, siding and much more—which lead to my career later on as a remodeler, designer and custom-home builder. I've seen both the good and the bad over the years, and as a result, I truly understand the process, the challenges and the strategies necessary for success. The good news is that with proper preparation, realistic expectations and the application of some basic strategies, you can find this to be an exciting and fun experience. My hope is that you and your family remember your renovation project for many years as a wonderful turning point in your lives. You'll also come out the other side with a beautiful home that enhances your financial security and the quality of your lives in many ways—and enjoy your own place in the American Dream.

Here are some suggested steps to prepare yourself for renovation success:

1. ***Schedule a family meeting.*** So let's get the kids together along with grandpa and grandma or anyone else who's going to be impacted by this project, and let's talk about exactly what we're going to be living through together. It's going to be a lot easier if everyone in the family is on the same page, recognizing that this is going to be challenging. The message is that if we work together, if we anticipate and plan ahead, we can survive. I encourage you to run through this list and discuss each point as a group.

2. *Realize the renovation is going to take longer than you'd like.* Accept this reality right up front. I referred earlier to the movie "The Money Pit," and unfortunately, remodeling can often be a lot like that. Each time Tom Hanks and Shelley Long, playing the young homeowners, would ask when the project would be finished, they were given the same answer: "Two weeks." And week after week, they remained two weeks away from completion.

3. *Expect things to go wrong.* That's the nature of construction. You've got a houseful of people running around trying to get all kinds of different work done at the same time. They're using noisy, dangerous tools, busting holes into walls and floors, and working on things that haven't been touched for many years. There are going to be surprises and mistakes and things going wrong. It's all part of the renovation game. So realize that there's no good to come from getting frustrated or angry over these setbacks, and there's only stress to come from worrying about things you can't control in any way. Millions of remodeling projects are undergone every year and somehow people do survive.

4. *Anticipate inconveniences and delays.* A remodeling project never seems to go as smoothly as we'd like, and as a result, almost never seems to get finished quite as soon as we'd like. And when you have your house full of contractors and everything torn up around you, it's going to change the way you live. You might reach a point where you feel you can't deal with the inconveniences any more. At that point take a deep breath, dig in, and realize that soon you'll be looking back on this experience and it won't be able to hurt you anymore.

5. *Agree that somehow life must go on.* Of course you'll need to adapt your life in some ways, but you're not going to put your entire life on the back shelf. You may have to go to work, kids may have to go to school and other critical things need to happen. The goal is to prepare yourself by asking, "How can we plan ahead now to minimize compromises in our life as we move forward?"

6. *Prepare for the kids and pets.* Think about how the construction activities might impact them. Do we have to move them around in the house? Do we have to make special provisions of some sort? Is it possible to find another home or location for them during the hours of construction activity? How can we keep them out of the way of the contractors and away from dust, noise or dirt?

7. *Make sure you have a first aid kit.* When you have construction materials and tools around, there are a lot of ways for someone to get hurt. There's usually someone in every family who has an almost magical ability to get hurt and sometimes even draw blood. Of course, construction workers get hurt now and then as well, so being prepared for this is a good idea.

8. *Plan realistic solutions for bathrooms and kitchens that may be out of service.* If your kitchen is only out of service for a day or two, you can certainly go out for breakfast or dinner. If this will occur over a longer term, you may want to set up a small temporary kitchen in another area of the house. If the entire family will be using one bathroom, you may need to create a schedule or some new rules to keep bloodshed to a minimum.

9. *Pack away fragile and valuable possessions.* This sounds like something that's pretty obvious, but I have been amazed to see homeowners leave these kinds of things right out in the open, just begging to be broken or stolen. It's well worth the extra effort to pack these things safely away to bring back out after all the construction workers have moved on to their next projects.

10. *Prepare for the dust.* I'm sure you'll agree dust can drive you out of your mind, especially if you're finicky about keeping things nice and clean. Cover up electronics, furniture and other valuables objects that aren't going to be removed from the construction area. You may want to seal off doorways and vents. It's amazing how construction going on in one area can take over the whole house. So plan ahead for that. Talk with your contractor about how you're going to keep sawdust, drywall dust and other airborne contaminants under control.

11. *Consider the impact of your project on your neighbors.* Think about the contractors, trucks and construction equipment coming and going, as well as all the noise and mess they make. There's usually some amount of in-convenience to your neighbors, so I encourage you to try to anticipate and minimize this however possible. I think it's a worthwhile idea to make a visit to your neighbors in advance. You may want to bring donuts, a pie or some cookies—or depending on the neighbors, maybe some beer or wine instead. Make them aware of what's coming up and let them know that you're going to do your best to make sure it doesn't negatively impact them. Show them you care, and encourage them to reach out to you directly at any time if there are

issues or concerns. Then cross your fingers and hope for the best.

12. *Plan some time away from the combat zone.* I know there's a desire to stay there to keep your eye on everything and make sure it all goes right, but depending on the length and the nature of the construction, you may want to plan an escape at some point. All that craziness can overwhelm your life. Maybe schedule a few days here and another few there to break up the insanity. You may not want to fly across the world in case you're needed for something in a hurry, but getting away from the chaos can be a very good thing.

13. *Demonstrate patience—and then even more patience.* Whether dealing with your family, your neighbors, the contractors or maybe even the guy at the gas station, realize that it's possible the stress could cause you to act in ways that are out of character. I encourage you to try and keep things in perspective, and to realize that even if things go wrong, even if it's a lot of pressure, even if you're sick of the mess, this is something that you are doing to better your life. All of this craziness will make sense in the end, providing a better home and future for you and your family.

14. *Realize the renovation is going to take longer than you'd like.* Yes, I know this is already on our list, but I feel it's worth repeating to make sure you're fully prepared for the fun and games.

Chapter 20

Surviving the Contractors

My next survival advice has to do with your day-to-day interaction with the contractors. Again, having spent many years running construction projects, I'll share some suggestions here I think you'll find helpful. Our goal is not only to end up with the finished home of our dreams, but to do so without any stress, violence or bloodshed over issues with our contractors. To that end, I offer the following suggestions:

1. *Do your due diligence.* Looking back to when you're choosing the contractors to bid on your project, it's important to determine whether they have a good track record and a good reputation. It's well worthwhile to take the time and make a few phone calls to talk to some past customers and other references. My advice here is to ask the contractor about work they've been doing in the area—what kind of projects and how things have come out. Let them tell you a little bit about the work they've done and then politely ask, "Could you give me these customer names and phone numbers? I'd really like the opportunity to talk with someone who has just gone through some major remodeling to hear any suggestions or advice they might have."

And if this a good contractor who truly does good work, gets along well with his customers, and follows through on things properly, there should be no hesitation to share those names and phone numbers. In my work as a contractor, I took a great deal of pride in the excellent relationships I built with my customers and their satisfaction with my work. I would offer new prospective customers not just a few references to call, but a complete list of customers for all the projects I had completed over the last several years. I think this made a strong statement to my prospects. I also feel there was a value connecting them with past customers who had survived the building or remodeling process successfully and were happy to have gone down that road.

2. *Remember that builders are people, too.* Even though contractors may seem like "rough and tumble" kind of people, they're really just like us in most ways. They're raising families, they're going to church, and they're going to work every

day to make the most of their lives. Most of them take pride in what they do, and even though they may not have graduated from business school or hold any professional degrees, they deserve our respect for their skills and experience.

3. *Show kindness and patience.* Every now and then I run into customers who decide that the only way things are going to go well is if they personally take charge of the construction project. They feel that using intimidation and being demanding will give them greater control over the situation. Unfortunately, most of the good contractors I know are not going to respond well to that kind of an attitude. And believe me, many of these contractors will find a way to turn the table on a rude or overly demanding customer. Remember, these are people who work very hard and are typically proud of their profession. A little kindness can go a long way.

4. *Don't allow them to push you around.* At the same time we're showing the contractors respect and patience, it's important we receive the same back from them. It's unfortunate that kindness can be perceived by some individuals as weakness. If you find that's the case in your contractor dealings at any point, it's important that you face it head on. If someone steps over the line into disrespectful communication or behavior, I believe it's essential to make it absolutely clear that this is not acceptable to you under any circumstances.

5. *Communicate with the McGimster.* If you search online for the term "McGimster," or look it up in any dictionary, you won't find it. "McGimster" is a term that was passed down to me by my father, who made it up himself one day. As a young Irishman working on construction sites back in his day, my father used to use this term to describe whoever was running the job. Working on projects when I was a boy, my father would let us take turns being in charge of what was happening next. So we'd be getting ready to start a project and he'd look around at us and say, "All right, who's going to be the McGimster today?" If we had a question about something, he'd look up and say, "Run it by the McGimster." Of course, for most of these projects, even when one of us had been given the role for the day, my father really was the McGimster. And we all respected that.

The point he was teaching us is that it's essential to have someone piloting the ship, driving the bus, or whatever analogy you'd like to use. Someone has to take charge, organize things, manage the details and be responsible for communications. The problem we can run into on our renovation project is communicating with whoever happens to be around the job that day. We can have different people coming and going, suppliers, subcontractors, inspectors and such, so it can be tempting to talk with anyone who happens to be there when we have a question or concern.

You need to determine right up front who's really the McGimster. I encourage you to have a clear understanding with the contractor regarding the proper channels for communications, how we track things in writing, how we finalize selections, changes and other matters.

6. *Keep your promises.* We expect the contractors and others we deal with in our lives to keep their promises. We expect them to follow through and do what they say they're going to do when they say they're going to do it. It's just as important we do the same. Whether finalizing selection information, visiting a supply house, processing documents for payment, or other activities related to the project, make it your mission to be someone they can count on. Otherwise, your delays can magnify themselves and a lack of trust can come about in the process, leading to other issues along the way.

7. *Stay the heck out of the way.* I can tell you as a contractor that a lot of well-meaning people love to stand around and visit, they like to help out, hold the ends of boards we're cutting, and just generally find ways to be part of the fun. Unfortunately, more often than not, all they're doing is slowing the process down. In spite of the best intentions, all they're doing is getting in the way and making it more difficult for us to get our work done. So if you don't have anything better to do at home, please just get the heck out of the house and come back later. If you offer, now and then we might find some something you can help with—more than likely a run to the hardware store for a widget or a gadget—but having a peanut gallery is not one of a contractors favorite things.

8. *Make notes of your questions or ideas.* You know you're going to come up with questions in the middle of the night, in the evening, when no one's around. Or maybe you come up with some cool idea one day and you're not going to see the McGimster until next week. Write the stuff down. Keep notes of those kinds of things so when you do have a conversation you can just go through the list and communicate more efficiently. Otherwise, you're calling or texting every two or three hours or every two or three days asking one question here, one question there. The more you stay organized, the better for everyone involved.

9. *Make decisions promptly and on time.* It's amazing to me how many people become so aggravated when the construction gets behind schedule a day or two. Yet, when it came to finalizing their choices of colors, finishes or other selections necessary to keep the project moving, the homeowners themselves were always behind schedule—sometimes as much as a week or two. Make it your mission to show respect to your contractors by making these decisions in a timely manner.

10. *Don't keep making changes.* Even though the contractor may have a process in place for possible changes, I highly recommend you do your very best not to make them. It's impossible to get the job done if we're changing every day. In the case of a renovation loan, this is even more critical since processing changes to the scope of work can cause issues for the lender relative to the funds in escrow, the appraisal value and other considerations. So make some well-thought-out decisions up front and live with them. There are millions of possible choices and no matter how many times you change your mind, there's no such thing as the perfect decision.

11. *Don't get "while you're at it" disease.* You may have never heard of this affliction, but it sometimes strikes innocent people at epidemic levels on construction sites. I've faced this dreaded disease for many years in my work as a contractor. It can manifest itself in many ways. For example, the electrician is working on some rough wiring and the customer pops over and asks, "Hey while you're at it, could you run some wiring over there and put in another switch?" Or someone asks the HVAC contractor, "While you're at it, could you run a gas line out the back of the house and over to that corner for my barbeque grill?"

It sure sounds like something really easy when you add that "while you're at it" line in there, but the reality is that it's usually not easy, it takes extra time and costs extra money. The appropriate question is, "How much will it cost if you were to add this extra work while you're already here on the project?" Contractors will appreciate it when you don't make them feel as if you're trying to take money out of their pockets.

When I was a boy, my father told me a story I've never forgotten:

The landlord of an apartment building awoke in the middle of the night to shouts of complaints from his tenants. It was a brutally cold winter evening, and the ancient boiler heating system had shut down again, leaving them freezing in their apartments. As he had done many times before, the landlord bundled up, trudged to the cellar and struggled for some time trying to get the big old monster to come back to life. Although the last thing he wanted to do was invest any more into it, exasperated, he finally called in "Bob the Boiler Man" to repair the beast.

Bob arrived in short order, and without any words, set down his toolbox, and walked around the boiler slowly analyzing the situation at hand. Still silent, he returned to his toolbox and pulled out a small hammer. Then holding the hammer straight in front of him, Bob intently focused on a spot on the boiler, waited for the precise moment, suddenly swung it back and hit the machine with one loud smack. Miraculously, the boiler roared to life.

Bob pulled an invoice book from his pocket, scribbled on the page for a moment, and still not having spoken a word, handed an invoice to the landlord.

Studying the invoice, the landlord looked at him in disbelief. "You're charging me $101 for this? You haven't been here five minutes and all you did was hit it once with your hammer!"

Bob calmly responded, "I only charged you $1 for hitting with the hammer. The $100 was for knowing where to hit."

Chapter 21

Surviving the Construction Zone

Now that we've taken the steps to lay our foundation for success, and identified our strategies for surviving the contractors, I'd like to next share some suggestions to help you survive the construction zone itself. To cover this topic, I've prepared a list of questions you can ask yourself and discuss with your contractor before the start of construction. Finding good answers to each of these can benefit everyone working and living in the construction zone. I think you'll find most of this pretty much self-explanatory.

1. Who is responsible for controlling dust and cleaning up the messes?

2. Who's going to put plastic up on doorways, cover vents, etc.?

3. Who's going to cover furniture and other valuables?

4. What areas of the home are off limits or must be only accessed with special permission?

5. Is there a bathroom in the house that's available for use by the workers, or should we have a porta potty provided for that purpose?

6. What days and hours are reasonable for work?

7. How early can we have someone there using a chainsaw or making lots of noise and how late at night is that going to be acceptable?

8. Where will materials and tools be kept?

9. Where will buckets and brushes be cleaned?

10. At any point during the renovation should we anticipate dangerous fumes or odors?

11. Are there any times we should plan to leave the house for a few days?

12. How will the grass and landscaping be protected?

13. Who's responsible if damage to the driveway or the landscaping occurs?

14. How will interior items such as furniture, flooring, cabinets and appliances be protected and who will be responsible for any damage that may occur?

15. Who will be responsible for unlocking and locking the house when you're not there?

16. Who will provide advance notice on turning off the water, the power, the heat or other inconveniences?

17. Where will the workers park?

18. Where will deliveries be made?

19. Is loud music and profanity on the jobsite expected or considered acceptable?

I remember promising a customer one time that I would make sure there was no loud music and profanity on the jobsite. They laughed and told me they actually enjoyed loud music and profanity. Go figure. So you never know what's going to make people happy, but running through this list together with your contractor can make a big difference in establishing a higher level of cooperation and minimizing friction.

Chapter 22

One Dream at a Time

This chapter brings us to the end of our journey together. We're sure you'll agree we've covered a lot of ground. And we hope what we've shared has opened your eyes to new possibilities and inspired you to consider leveraging the power of the FHA 203k program to change your life in a positive way.

Remembering back to the beginning of this book, do you think it's possible you might be sitting around with your children and grand-children someday telling them your own 203k success story? We certainly hope so. Here are similar stories of a few who changed their lives through the power of the 203k:

Instant Equity – *A home sits on the market in Northern California for more than 18 months because the interior is torn up with damage to electrical, plumbing and the flooring throughout. Most REALTORS® haven't bothered to show the home since it looks like such a mess. A few prospective buyers visited the home at some point, but couldn't imagine how they could possibly pull together the money for both the down payment and the needed repairs. Of course, none of them were aware of the FHA 203k.*

Finally, a resourceful loan officer prepared a simple breakdown showing how the repairs could be folded into a 203k mortgage. He brought in a contractor to provide repair estimates and asked the listing agent to estimate the value of the home after repairs. His numbers reflected the low down payment required as well as the fact that based on the new listing price, buyers could make repairs and enjoy new equity of almost $100,000!

The listing agent then held another open house sharing the lender's cost breakdown, and the house was almost immediately sold to a lucky young family. Although other buyers and agents had been ignoring this property, by purchasing it with a 203k, this turned out to be one of the best investments in town.

Becoming a Landlord – *A young man had dreamed for years of investing in rental properties to build his financial future, but still had not yet owned his first home. In his search for solutions, he found* **rebuildusa.com** *and became excited about the possibility of finally making his dream come true. Our support team introduced him to a real estate agent and loan officer from our national 203k Specialist network to help him explore things further.*

As it turned out, his credit report came back with negative information, so with the lender's guidance, he set to work improving his credit scores. In the meantime, his agent found a bank-owned, three-unit property that needed some long overdue repairs and improvements, but was in a good neighborhood at a reasonable asking price. The building had a great deal of character, but simply needed some love to bring it back to life.

With an accepted offer, our friend got busy assembling his funds for the required down payment, which including some money gifted from several family members. Several months later, he became the proud owner of not just his first home, but his first investment property where he enjoyed rental income each month to help cover his mortgage payments and ownership expenses. Using 203k renovation funds, he soon repainted, replaced windows and brought back the beauty of this once proud property.

He now had his piece of the American Dream, and was on his path to building his real estate empire. This would simply have not been possible without the 203k and the support of professionals to help him pull it all together!

We've all seen the long-term benefits of homeownership enjoyed by so many Americans over past decades. Think about how many people have built greater financial stability as appreciation over time brought them an amazing return on their investment. For many, it's become the very foundation of a secure financial future as they move into the twilight of their lives.

Unfortunately, too many people today feel they'll never enjoy a similar opportunity. Too many feel that homeownership is entirely beyond their reach. Yet, as a result of your new awareness of the power of the 203k, we hope you now have a very different perspective—realizing that it's entirely possible for millions of Americans to make this dream come true.

Is it easy for anyone to make this happen? Certainly not. The renovation loan process is not for the faint-of-heart. There are some folks who simply do not have the disposition, self-discipline or patience to pull this all together. If you're someone who flips out over the least little setback or problem, then you're not an ideal candidate for a ride on the 203k train.

At the same time, it's not an impossible mission either. As you consider the process and strategies we've shared, we hope you realize that with patience, planning, and the support of the right professionals to help you navigate the waters, you can be one of many thousands of people who enjoy renovation loan success every year.

We know that most of the really great things we achieve in our lives don't come easily. Our greatest accomplishments and significant goals we reach most often come about through hard work and perseverance. Making your homeownership dreams come true is one of these kinds of achievements, so it's unlikely that we'll cross this finish line without making some sacrifices and overcoming challenges along the way.

Teresa and I believe that today represents only the beginning as it relates to the future of renovation loans. Along with us, many other real estate industry experts expect renovation loans to someday be used by hundreds of thousands across America every year. With a massive, aging housing stock across the country, it just makes sense that this powerful financial solution will be used long into the future.

Again, we want to emphasize the importance of our mission as it relates to increasing homeownership and contributing to greater financial security for individuals and families. Further, we hope as these homes are renovated one by one, we see older neighborhoods coming back to life, and newer communities maintaining their beauty far into the future. In the process, we all make a contribution to the health of our housing industry and our economy overall.

Most importantly, as homes and neighborhoods are repaired and renewed, people can live with a greater sense of pride, community and security. Rather than being surrounded by blight and crime, children can grow up in an environment that contributes to their self-respect and ultimately leads to more positive, productive lives. As a result, all of us can enjoy an even greater future.

> *The greatest "best kept secret" of all is the fact that as we rebuild our homes and neighborhoods, we are truly Rebuilding America One Dream at a Time!*

We hope what we've shared in this book will have a positive, lasting impact on your life and we thank you for sharing our message with others as well.

All our best,
Dennis and Teresa Walsh

203k Renovation Loan Glossary

203k Appraisal – To meet requirements for a 203k appraisal, the appraiser uses the scope of work and cost estimates from the contractor to determine a "subject to" or "after-improved value" of the home.

203k Consultant (HUD Consultant) – An individual meeting criteria established by the FHA to provide specific inspection, work write-up and cost estimating services to lenders and homebuyers during the approval and renovation phases of a 203k project. FHA-approved 203k Consultants are listed in an online HUD database and are selected by the lender as required.

"As-Is" Value - An estimate of the value of a property, typically by an FHA-approved appraiser, in its current state prior to renovation. This is required when using a 203k for refinance.

Assumable Mortgage – If the original mortgagor chooses to sell a home with an assumable mortgage, a qualified buyer can purchase the home "assuming" the balance of the current mortgage without having to secure his or her own mortgage. This becomes particularly beneficial when the original mortgage was secured at a rate lower than that available at the time of assumption.

Borrower's Acknowledgment – A HUD form required to be signed by buyers securing 203k financing, detailing specifics of handling and distribution of the renovation funds by the lender.

Closeout Requirements – The lender must follow a specific procedure and package specific documents to receive final approval and endorsement of a loan by the FHA.

Construction Draw – As work is completed on a construction project, the contractor may periodically submit a request for payment known as a "draw request." This payment would represent a percentage of the total relative to the percentage of work completed.

Construction Inspection – This is commonly used to refer to a visit to a construction project by a building inspector of some sort, whether a local official or an inspector hired by one of the parties of the construction contract. A lender, for example, will hire an inspector to visit the site to inspect the quality and completion of work prior to issuance of funds for a draw request.

Contingency Reserve – To allow for unforeseen expenses, a percentage of the total estimated cost of construction is sometimes held in an escrow account as a financial backup. Depending on the nature of the project, some 203k loans require a contingency reserve while others do not. Unused contingency funds are typically applied to the mortgage principal at the completion of the renovation portion of a 203k project.

Draw Request – This is a document submitted by the contractor to request an inspection and the subsequent release of funds relative to the completed portion of the project.

Energy Efficient Mortgage (EEM) – This mortgage can be added to a 203k or other FHA mortgage to provide funds beyond the FHA loan limits and the buyers' approved loan amount for "cost effective" energy improvements. Based on an inspection and analysis by a certified HERS Rater, qualifying improvements must save enough energy to pay for themselves over the expected life of the improvement.

Eligible Repairs – The FHA stipulates specific repairs and improvements as eligible for use of funds provided by a 203k loan. The eligible improvements differ depending on whether using a Standard or Streamline 203k.

Energy Audit – A site inventory and descriptive record of features impacting the energy use in a building. This includes, but is not limited to, all building component descriptions (locations, areas, orientations, construction attributes and energy transfer characteristics).

Evidence of Insurance – Contractors who provide renovation services for a 203k project must provide evidence of insurance to the satisfaction of the 203k lender.

Eligible Repairs – A specific list of repairs and improvements are qualified for use of renovation funds provided through each of the versions of the 203k.

Federal Housing Administration (FHA) – Established in 1934 to improve housing conditions and ownership opportunities for Americans, and operates today under HUD, offering insured mortgages in various forms.

FHA 203K Loan – An FHA-insured loan program that provides funds for both the purchase and renovation of a home packaged into a single mortgage loan.

FHA-Approved Home Inspector – Inspectors meeting criteria for approval by the FHA are featured in a searchable online database on the HUD website.

FHA Endorsement – Mortgage loans meeting specific requirements are accepted by the FHA under one of its insured mortgage loan programs. This acceptance is known as an endorsement of the loan and insures the lender in the event the mortgagor would default on the mortgage loan.

FHA Loan – The FHA does not actually provide mortgage funds, but instead, provides lenders with insurance that protects them against losses in the event of homeowner mortgage default.

FHA Loan Limits – Limits on the maximum amount of loan funds available to a borrower relative to housing costs in a given area. In areas of the country with lower home values, limits are currently set at a maximum of $271,000, while in other areas, these limits go as high as $729,750.

FHA Standard 203k – Is intended for more complicated projects that involve structural changes, such as room additions, exterior grading and landscaping, or renovation that would prohibit you from occupying the residence. A Standard 203k is also necessary if your project requires engineering or architectural drawings.

FHA Streamline 203k – Designed for less extensive improvements and for projects that will not exceed a total of $35,000 in renovation and related expenses. This version does not require the use of a consultant, architect and engineer or as many inspections as the Standard 203k.

Final Survey – If site improvements or additions to the structure are made during renovation, there may be a requirement for a final or "as-built" survey to be conducted for issuance of the occupancy permit.

Good Neighbor Next Door – A HUD program that offers HUD REO homes for a five-day window to local firefighters, law enforcement officers, emergency medical technicians and school teachers at a 50 percent discount off the acquisition value of the property.

HERS Rater – Individuals who are certified through specific training to be qualified to conduct a HERS energy analysis of a home. HERS stands for Home Energy Rating System, which is used to measure the relative energy efficiency of a home against the HERS Index. A HERS energy analysis is required to qualify improvements for inclusion into an Energy Efficient Mortgage (EEM).

Holdback – A practice more common in commercial construction than residential, where a percentage of payment is withheld from each draw distributed to contractors during the construction process. Under certain conditions, holdbacks are required on 203k projects, typically in the amount of 10 percent of funds disbursed. At completion and final acceptance by owner, holdback funds are then released.

Home Ownership Center (HOC) – There are four HOCs, each providing coverage for a different region of the U.S., providing lender support for FHA loan programs.

Homeowner/Contract Agreement – A HUD document offered as a sample of an agreement to be used between the homeowner and the renovation contractor(s). At a minimum, an agreement should be used that identifies parties of the contract, scope of work, all related costs, a one-year warranty and an arbitration clause in the event of disputes.

Department of Housing and Urban Development (HUD) – The Federal agency responsible for national policy and programs that address America's housing needs, improve and develop the nation's communities, and enforce fair housing laws.

HUD Consultant (203k Consultant) – An individual meeting criteria established by the FHA to provide consultant services to lenders and homebuyers during both the approval and renovation phases of a 203k project. FHA-approved 203k Consultants are listed in an online HUD database and are selected by the lender as required, typically on Standard 203k loans only.

Identity-of-Interest – This describes a requirement by the FHA for certification by homebuyers so that no family or business relationship exists between them and the sellers of the property. The FHA also requires certification by 203k Consultants that no identity of interest exists between them and any other parties to the transaction.

Ineligible Repairs – Specific list of repairs and improvements that are not allowed for each of the versions of the 203k.

Insurance of Advances – At the time of loan closing, the FHA endorses the total loan, including the renovation funds which are at this time placed into escrow. This means that the total loan is insured in advance of those funds being disbursed for renovation work on the project.

LTV (Loan-To-Value) Ratio – This is a ratio between the mortgage loan and the appraised value of the property used as a key component of the loan approval process. A typical FHA insured loan allows an LTV of 96.5 percent, which translates to a down payment requirement of 3.5 percent.

Mandatory Repairs – To qualify for FHA-insured financing, a home must meet HUD minimum standards, which refer to specific conditions relative to health, safety, energy efficiency and durability. A home that does not meet these minimum standards must have specific mandatory repairs done to allow for FHA endorsement.

Maximum Mortgage Worksheet – A HUD document used to calculate the various numbers related to a mortgage loan, including appraised value, as-improved value, closing costs, etc., to calculate the maximum qualifying mortgage loan amount for a specific property.

Minimum Repair Cost Threshold – On the Standard 203k, a minimum of $5,000 in repairs must be made to the property.

Mixed-Use Property – This refers to a property that combines a residential unit or units with space allocated for commercial or retail use. The FHA 203k can be used for mixed-use properties with up to four units of residential, providing the owner occupies one unit as a primary residence.

Mortgage Insurance Premium – Abbreviated as "MIP," this is an insurance premium added to the costs of the loan to provide insurance to the lender against losses that may be incurred in the event the owner would default on the mortgage loan.

Mortgagee – This is the term used by HUD to describe the lender.

Mortgagor – Refers to the homeowner who secures and is responsible for repayment of the mortgage loan.

Mortgagor Letter of Completion – A HUD document required to be signed by the homeowners following the completion of renovation to confirm their acceptance of the work and their acknowledgement that final payment will be released to the contractor(s).

Occupancy Permit – A permit issued by a local building department, health department, and/or other required government division accepting the completion of construction and authorizing the owners to occupy the property.

Owner-Occupant – The FHA requires that 203k loans are issued for properties that will be occupied by the mortgagor as a primary residence.

PFC – Prepaid Finance Charges

POC – Paid Outside of Closing

Qualifying Ratios – Several ratios are used by lenders to determine the amount of mortgage loan affordable to specific buyers. These commonly include the ratio between the monthly mortgage payment (PITI) and the buyer's monthly income, as well as the ratio between the monthly mortgage payment and total monthly payments on outstanding installment debt.

Rehabilitation Escrow Account – At the closing of a 203k loan, funds are disbursed for the purchase of the home, and renovation funds are set up in a separate escrow account to be disbursed to contractors in conformance with the Renovation Loan Agreement.

Scope of Work – Sometimes referred to as "work write-up" or "project specifications," this document provides the details of the renovation work to be completed under the terms of the contract.

Self-Help Arrangement – The FHA allows certain renovation work to be performed under the terms of a 203k loan by the homeowners. Referred to as a "Self-Help Arrangement," this is only allowed where homeowners can demonstrate professional expertise in the applicable trade or activity.

Streamline 203k – A version of the 203k introduced in 2005 to offer a simpler, less costly alternative to the original version of the 203k. The Streamline 203k is limited to renovation that does not require structural work or architectural and engineering drawings, and allows for total renovation costs not to exceed $35,000.

"Subject-to" Appraisal – This refers to an appraiser's estimate of the value of the home after completion of improvement specified in the Scope of Work documents. In other words, this appraisal is "subject to" the completion of improvements to the property.

Glossary of Construction Terms

A

Access Panel – Removable panel that allows access to plumbing or electrical connections, such as below a platform tub.

Acoustical Ceiling – Ceiling made up of materials that absorb sound to reduce the transfer of noise in a building.

Admixtures – Materials that are mixed into concrete to somehow change the nature of the mix, such as color or a curing accelerator used in cold weather.

Adobe – Clay soil used to create bricks that are sun-dried and used for constructing walls.

Aggregate – Gravel, stones, shells or other solid materials that are added to the concrete mix for strength or aesthetic purposes.

Air Quality – Measurement of the level of contamination of air in the building due to the buildup of chemicals and odors from building materials and occupants.

Air-vapor Barrier – Material used to eliminate the passage of air and moisture through walls, floors and ceilings, most commonly a layer of polyethylene plastic installed behind the drywall or below a concrete slab.

Anchor Bolts – Treaded metal bolts that are installed in the concrete at the top of a foundation, used to secure the wood plates that connect to floors and walls.

APA-rated – Rating given by the American Plywood Association that established the correct use of panel materials, such as plywood and waferboard.

Apron – Interior trim molding applied below a window stool.

Architect – Individual who designs and oversees building construction, usually used to refer to someone who is registered and licensed by the American Institute of Architects.

Ash Dump – Metal door that opens in the bottom of a fireplace to allow ashes to be "dumped" to a hollow ashpit below.

Asphalt Shingles – Roofing material made up of a mineral fiber mat that is impregnated with asphalt for waterproofing and covered with a decorative aggregate material.

Astragal – Narrow wood molding usually installed vertically between double doors.

Azimuth – Horizontal angle used in surveying to lay out the boundaries of a parcel of land relative to the directions of the compass.

B

Back Band – Separate, outermost trim piece that is used outside the casing around an interior window or door opening. This is a traditional colonial detail.

Backfill – Material such as dirt or gravel used to fill in the open area around a foundation, also the act of filling in this area.

Backsplash – Material applied to the vertical area above a sink or countertop to protect the wall finish from moisture.

Baffles, Insulation – Treated cardboard or light plastic pieces installed between rafters directly below the roof sheathing to maintain an airspace for ventilation above the ceiling insulation.

Balloon Framing – Framing method where exterior studs run continuously from the sill plate at the foundation to the top wall plate at the eaves of the roof, very seldom used today.

Baluster – One of the vertical components repeated underneath a stair or porch railing.

Balustrade – Stair or porch railing.

Barrel Vault – Upside-down, U-shaped design used at a vaulted ceiling.

Baseboard – The interior molding installed at the bottom of a wall.

Base Molding – Another term used to describe the baseboard.

Base Shoe – Strip of molding installed along the bottom of the baseboard, used most often in areas with hardwood, ceramic tile or marble floors.

Battens – Thin strips of wood applied over seams in wider boards, usually in a vertical application to create board and batten siding.

Batts – Insulation material manufactured in varying widths and thickness to allow for easy installations between rafters and studs, also called blankets.

Bay Window – Three-sided, angled window configuration that projects from the walls of a building.

Beam – Large piece of built-up lumber, timber, metal, stone or other structural material installed horizontally in a building to support structural loads.

Bearing wall – Wall supporting loads from above, including joists, rafters or other walls.

Beltboard – An exterior trim board installed horizontally directly below the soffit area.

Bevel Siding – Siding material that is triangular in shape and installed horizontally with each piece overlapping the piece below.

Bid Drawings – Architectural drawings created for the purpose of securing bids or cost estimates from contractors and suppliers.

Blind Nailing – Nail installed so that the head is covered by another piece of finish material and therefore not visible after completion.

Blocking – Short lengths of wood installed perpendicular to studs, joists and rafters to provide additional structural strength or to provide support for the installation of hardware during the finish.

Board & Batten – Vertical wood siding consisting of wide boards placed side-by-side with narrow batten strips that cover the joints.

Boiler Heating – Heating system that uses boilers to heat water that is then pumped through pipes and radiators to heat the air.

Boundary Survey – Survey that establishes the corners of a property and often includes stakes and ribbons to clearly identify property lines.

Brick Veneer – Full-thick brick that is used as the exterior finish on a wood frame building.

Bridging – Solid or crisscrossed boards used between joists to add additional strength to a floor system.

Brown Coat – Layer of coarse plaster applied beneath the finish coat in interior plaster work or exterior stucco.

Building Orientation – Placement of the building on the site relative to the weather, sunlight, views or other considerations.

Building Permits – Series of documents and approvals issued by various government offices that are required prior the start of construction.

Building Systems – Various combinations and methods of utilizing materials and labor, often using factory-built components, to create a building, such as panelized or modular construction.

Built-up Roofing – Combination of sheet materials, adhesives, waterproofing membranes and sometimes aggregates to create a roofing system; most often used on flat or low-slope roofs.

Bulkheads – Another term used for interior soffits built above wall cabinets or vanity areas.

Bullnose – Finish material applied to an edge, such as a countertop or step.

Butyl – Type of caulk used to ensure waterproof seams between building materials.

C

CAD – "Computer-aided-drafting" systems used by builders and designers to create architectural drawings.

Cantilever – Beam or section of floor that extends beyond the wall below.

Cased Opening – Opening between rooms without a door that is trimmed with wood jambs and casing; considered an upgrade from a drywall-wrapped opening.

Casement Window – Window hinged along one vertical side that opens and closes similar to a door.

Casing – The molding installed around a door or window opening.

Cathedral Ceiling – Ceiling with two sides sloping toward the center of the room.

Cedar – Reddish-brown wood that is used as exterior siding and roofing due to its ability to resist decay and rot in exposed conditions.

Cement – Material made by grinding limestone and clay to a fine powder, usually mixed with water and sand to make mortar or by adding aggregates to make concrete.

Ceramic Tile – Durable, but brittle, tiles used for walls, floors and roofs that are created from clay heated to very high temperatures.

Check Valve – Valve used in a pipe that carries fluids to allow movement of the fluid in only one direction.

Chemically Treated – Usually refers to wood products that are treated with chemicals to resist decay or to slow fire damage.

Chimney – Vertical structure or flue that allows the passage of smoke and gases from a furnace or fireplace into the air safely above a roof.

Chimney Cap – Metal or masonry material used at the top of a chimney or flue to prevent water from leaking into the chimney structure.

Cladding – Material applied to another material to change its appearance or ability to resist wear or decay, such as in vinyl- or aluminum-clad doors and windows.

Clapboard – Narrow, beveled boards applied overlapping horizontally as exterior siding, also called bevel or lap siding.

Clay Tile – Roofing or floor tiles created by heating natural clay materials; also sometimes used to describe drainage pipes or "drain tiles" made of this material.

Cleanout – Opening that allows access to pipes, drain lines or an ashdump for cleaning.

Clerestory – Vertical wall that rises above a section of roof with windows installed to bring natural light into a building.

Closed Valley – Valley construction where shingles are overlapped at the center of the valley.

Collar Tie – Horizontal framing member installed above the ceiling joists between rafters to strengthen the roof system.

Column – Vertical component of a structure, usually made of wood, concrete or metal, used to support loads above or for aesthetic purposes.

Concrete – Building material created by mixing cement, sand, gravel, water and other admixtures that is poured in place wet and then through a chemical reaction, cures or hardens to a solid.

Control Joints – Small cuts or joints trowelled into the surface of a concrete slab in a decorative pattern to attempt to "control" the direction of cracks that appear over time.

Corner Bead – Metal or plastic piece applied where drywall meets at a right angle to provide a rigid, straight line behind the joint compound.

Corner Braces – Diagonal lengths of wood or metal applied at the corners of exterior walls behind the sheathing to provide structural reinforcement.

Cornice – Horizontal moldings that project from the face of a wall to create a crown or cap.

Cove Molding – Molding with a concave curve used for various trim purposes.

Crawl Space – A foundation system that raises a wood floor several feet above grade, providing a low space beneath the floor for access to mechanicals.

Creosote – Oily, brownish liquid from coal tar that is applied to wood to act as a preservative.

Cricket – Small, gable roof-shaped structure that is installed above a chimney to divert rainwater around the chimney.

Cripple Studs – Short studs installed below a window sill or above a header to provide backing for the wall finish material.

Crown Molding – Molding typically used at the intersection of a wall and a ceiling. Simpler crowns are single strips of wood molded in a decorative shape. More ornate crown moldings are built up of several separate molding pieces.

Cupola – Small structure, usually rectangular with a peaked roof, built on top of the roof of a building, sometimes for ventilation, sometimes for decorative purposes.

Curtain Drain – French drain installed at an elevation above the leach field area of a septic system to collect surface water before it runs over the leach field and carries effluent to neighboring properties.

Cut-and-Fill Computation – Calculations made to determine the proper amount of soil to excavate from a basement and the corresponding placement of soil around the basement on the finished site.

D

Damper – Adjustable metal plate in the flue of a furnace, fireplace or ductwork to control the flow of air or exhaust.

Dead Bolt – Lock installed above the handset with a solid bolt for additional security.

Dead Load – Engineering calculation that measures the average weight of the structural components in a floor or roof system.

Dentil – Molding that consists of repeated tooth-like blocks usually applied below an overhang or as a component of a built-up crown molding.

Distribution Panel – Electrical panel that distributes electricity from the main to various circuits throughout the building; typically holds banks of circuit breakers.

Dormer – Smaller structure made up of three walls, a window and a roof that projects through the main roof of a building.

Double Glazing – Assembly of two panels of glass with a narrow air space between them installed in a door or a window to provide increased energy efficiency over a single-pane design.

Double-hung Window – Window with both an upper and lower sash that can be slid vertically to open and close.

Drain Tile – Term used to describe perforated plastic or clay pipes installed below grade to collect water in the soil and carry it away to a storm sewer or surface runoff.

Drip Edge – Thin metal flashing applied to the edges of the roof sheathing to direct rain water down to the gutters or siding.

Dropped Ceiling – False ceiling installed below an existing ceiling, often used to hide exposed pipes or ductwork.

Drywall – Paper-covered gypsum board used for the finish interior wall surface. Joints are concealed with paper tape and plaster-like joint compound.

Ducts – Manufactured in galvanized metal, fiberglass board and flexible plastic, ducts are used to distribute conditioned air from heating and air-conditioning systems, and to vent exhaust fans in kitchens and bathrooms.

E

Eaves – Lowest edge of a roof, typically above an exterior wall.

Efflorescence – White, powdery substance that sometimes appears on brick walls.

Elevations – Describes architectural drawings that provide a representation of a vertical surface, such as the exterior of a building.

Excavation – Process of using heavy earth-moving equipment to dig areas for foundations and other site work.

Expansion Joint – Joint constructed in concrete slabs filled with a flexible, compressible material to allow for the expansion and contraction of the concrete relative to changes in temperature.

Exterior Elevation – Describes the finished exterior of a building or architectural drawing that shows these finished exterior views.

F

Face Brick – Brick applied to create a finish over a structural wall or chimney.

Fascia – Collectively describes the various finish materials and trims that occur along the edges of a roof.

Fiberglass – Material typically used in a loose or batt configuration for insulation purposes.

Filter Fabric – Heavy fabric sheet installed below base stone in a driveway or over the gravel around a foundation to minimize contamination from fine soil and mud.

Finish Carpentry – Process of installing interior doors, cabinets, moldings and finish hardware.

Finish Nails – Fine nails with small heads used to apply finish moldings and trim materials.

Firebox – Opening inside of a fireplace, lined with fire brick, where the fire burns.

Firebrick – Light-colored brick used inside the firebox.

Fire-rated – Rating established for building materials that represents their performance during a fire; required for certain materials by building codes.

Firestopping – Horizontal framing installed between studs to minimize the possibility that fire can pass quickly up the wall cavities.

Fixed Glass – Glazing installed in a door or window without a moveable sash.

Flashing – Materials used to eliminate the passage of water at roof areas, sidewalls, windows and doors, usually made of metal.

Flight – Uninterrupted series of steps between floors or between a floor and a landing.

Flood Plain – Geographic area designated by the Army Corps of Engineers as being potentially subject to flooding at some time in the future.

Floor Joists – Horizontal framing members, usually 2x8's or 2x10's, used to create the structural framework of a floor.

Flue – Terra cotta or metal lining for a chimney or furnace vent.

Fluting – Vertical decorative grooves in a column typically used at fireplaces or entry doors.

Footing (or Footers) – Structural component at the base of the foundation that transfers the loads of the building to the soil below. Footings (or footers) are usually constructed of concrete poured directly on stable, bearing soils.

Forced-air System – System of plenums and ductwork where fans move conditioned air through a building.

Forms – Wood, plastic or metal assembled to support wet concrete before it cures.

Foundation – Combination of components below grade, including footings, basement walls, crawl space walls, columns, piers, pilings, etc., that supports the structure.

Framing – Term applied to the process and materials used to create the rough structure of the building.

French Drain – Trench filled with gravel with some form of drain pipes installed at the bottom to collect surface water away from a building.

Furring – Wood strips applied to provide either an air space or to provide a nailing material for the installation of sidings and finishes over concrete, block or foam materials.

G

Gable – Vertical, triangular-shaped area of wall that occurs where the ridge of a roof meets the end of the structure.

Gable Roof – Triangular-shaped roof that results when two sloping roof planes meet along a horizontal edge.

Galvanized – Metal coated with rust-resistant zinc.

Gambrel Roof – Ridged roof with dual slopes on each side of the ridge, the lower slope being of a higher pitch.

Glazing – Term used to describe various types and combinations of glass used in a window, door or skylight.

Glue-lam – Short for "glue-laminated," describes structural components, most often beams, made up of pieces of dimension lumber glued together.

Grout – Mortar-like material, usually colored, used to fill space between floor and wall tiles.

Gypsum – White material used in the production of plaster, joint compounds and drywall which is sometimes referred to as gypsum board.

H

Header – Structural component that carries loads across an opening, typically constructed of standard lumber, laminated wood products or steel.

Hearth – Horizontal, non-flammable finish surface installed at the front of the fireplace below the firebox opening.

Heat Pump – Device that utilizes a compressor system to heat and cool a building.

Hip Roof – Roof shape that results from triangular roof surfaces that slope upward, away from the eaves.

Hollow-core Door – Door used most often at interior locations constructed with a relatively thin layer of veneer on each face and a lightly reinforced hollow core.

Hose Bib – Exterior water faucet.

House Wrap – Fabric-like materials that are wrapped around the exterior sheathing of a building to eliminate air infiltration while still allowing moisture to escape from the wall cavity, can significantly reduce energy costs.

Hurricane Clips – Various types of metal anchors and connectors that are used to securely connect structural components in a building to increase resistance to damage from storms and wind.

Hydrostatic Pressure – Moisture in the soil that builds up, creating pressure against foundation walls.

I

Infiltration – Movement or leaking of air through the exterior shell of a building, often measured in "air changes" which represent the complete replacement of interior, conditioned air with air from outside the structure.

Insulating Sheathing – Various types of exterior sheathing materials that are designed to reduce energy loss.

J

Jack Stud – Stud at each side of an opening that is cut short to support the header above.

Jamb – Finish material applied around the inside of a door or window opening.

Joist – Horizontal framing members that support a floor or ceiling joists, headers and beams.

K

Knee Wall – Low wall in an attic or half-story space.

L

Laminated Veneer Lumber – Sometimes called a "micro-lam," structural components, usually used as beams or headers, made up of thin veneer layers much the same as plywood.

Lap Siding – Exterior siding applied horizontally and "lapped" over the board below, such as clapboard siding.

Lath – Material installed as a backing material for plaster, stucco and sometimes tile installation, lath is usually a metal mesh, but sometimes rough wood strips or gypsum board.

Lintel – Used interchangeably with the term "header," a lintel is a horizontal component that carries loads from above across an opening, such as a steel angle in brick work.

Live Load – Engineering term that describes changeable loads in a structure, usually calculated on a square-foot basis, such as loads from people, snow or winds.

Low-E Glazing – Various types and combinations of glazing that utilize glass, reflective films, suspended films and gas injected in the space between the glass to reduce energy loss.

M

Mansard Roof – Roof shape with two slopes on each side, the upper slope being a very flat pitch, and the lower slope, which often covers the side wall of the upper floor area, being a very steep pitch.

Mantel – Shelf assembly, usually with a crown mold below it, that is constructed above a door, window, or most commonly, a fireplace opening.

Marine Plywood – Plywood panels constructed with special waterproof adhesives to allow material to stand up to extremely wet applications.

Masonry – Any construction that involves the use of stone, brick or block materials, such as exterior veneer, foundations or fireplaces.

Mechanicals – Term used to describe the trades or work involved in the installation of plumbing, electrical and HVAC systems.

Metal Door – Refers to a door constructed with a thin metal skin, usually embossed with decorative panels, over a core of insulating foam.

Metal Lath – Metal mesh material that is attached to walls, floors and ceilings as base for plaster, mortar for stone work or thinset for tile and marble installation.

Miter Joints – Joints in lumber or moldings where diagonals are cut to fit the pieces around an angle, such as at the corners of windows and doors.

Modular Construction – The construction of a building using sections that are built in a factory and then assembled together in the field to complete the structure. Modules usually include finished interior and exterior components as well as mechanicals that are spliced where modules meet.

Mortar – Various materials that are used to bond together masonry materials, such as brick and stone, normally a mixture of cement, sand and water.

Mortise – Rectangular hole cut into wood that receives a tenon from another piece to make a connection; used in furniture and post-and-beam framing.

Mullions – Vertical strips that separate panes of glass in a door or window; also used to describe removable grills or grids to create the appearance of separate panes.

N

Newel Post – Post that supports a hand rail at the landing or starting step of a staircase.

Nominal Dimensions – Used to describe various sizes of lumber typically used in construction, although actual dimensions are different, i.e., a 2x4 is actually 1 1/2" x 3 1/2".

Nosing – Projecting edge that trims a step.

O

Open Riser – Stair construction that uses no riser between treads for an open appearance.

Open Soffit – Exterior soffit construction where no finish material is installed to cover the overhang area, leaving the tails of the rafters exposed.

Open Stringer – Staircase construction where stair treads extend with a nosing over the decorative stringer. Balusters are then installed directly into the treads.

Open Valley – Valley construction at the roof where shingles are cut back at each side of the valley to expose the metal flashing material.

Oriented Strand Board – Waferboard-type panel that uses longer wafers or strands that are oriented to the length of the panel, creating a directional panel that offers more strength than conventional waferboard.

P

Panel Clips – Small metal clips installed at the edges of roof sheathing panels between roof trusses to eliminate misalignment of the edges and provide an expansion space.

Panelized Construction – Building construction system that utilizes panels, or wall sections, that are assembled in a factory for quicker, more accurate assembly in the field.

Panels – Term used to describe materials manufactured in 4x8 and 4x9 sizes, such as plywood, waferboard, oriented strand board and particle board.

Particle Board – Panel material constructed from fine wood particles, like sawdust, and glue, typically used as a structural backing material for laminate cabinets and countertops.

Passive Solar Heating – Building design that maximizes heat absorption from the sun without active or powered systems.

Pediment – Ornamental triangular trim assembly or gable typically used above doors and windows and as decorative elements at the front of buildings.

Pier – Masonry or concrete column used to support a floor or porch.

Pilaster – Rectangular column, most often structural, that projects slightly from a wall.

Piling – Vertical structural component buried below a building as foundational support, usually pressure-treated wood posts, steel columns or concrete.

Pitch – Slope of a roof, usually described as a ratio between rise and run.

Plaster – Mixture of lime or cement with sand and water that is applied in a wet paste and then dries hard as a finish for walls and ceilings.

Plat – Parcel of land, or a drawing showing dimensions and details of a parcel or group of parcels.

Plate – Horizontal framing members at the top and bottom of a wall. "Plate height" is often used to refer to the ceiling height of a room.

Platform Framing – Most popular system of frame construction. First floor platform is constructed, then walls are built on this, then second floor platform followed by second floor walls; differs from balloon framing.

Plinth – Square block used as a trim at the base of a column or a casing.

Plywood – Structural panel material constructed of thin layers, or veneers, of wood glued together, typically with alternating grain direction between layers.

Porch – Covered area attached to a building, open to the outside on at lease one side.

Porte Cochere – Exterior area covered by a roof that allows vehicles to drive through or park under; allows people to enter or exit vehicles protected from the rain.

Post-tension Concrete – Concrete slab construction used in areas with extreme expansive soils, involves the installation of metal cables at opposite directions in the slab which are then put in tension to eliminate cracking and separation due to soil movement.

Pre-cast Concrete – Building construction that uses concrete components for walls, floor and roof structure that are pre-cast in sections in a factory.

Pre-engineered Trusses – Structural components assembled in a factory used for floor and roof construction that utilize lumber or steel along with bracing and steel connector plates.

Preliminary Drawings – Architectural drawings used for the purpose of establishing the general design of a building before detailed, or working, drawings are finalized; usually used to determine preliminary cost estimates and secure owners' approval for final design.

Pressure-treated Wood – Lumber and plywood that is treated with a chemical preservative for exterior or extreme moisture conditions, most commonly used in residential construction for exterior decks and sill plates at grade.

Protection Board – Various types of sheet materials used around a foundation to protect waterproofing membranes from damage; often also provide additional insulation to the foundation.

PVC – Common plastic material (polyvinyl chloride) used for drain pipes, such as footer drains and waste lines.

Q

Quarry Tile – Machine-made, unglazed tile often used for floors.

Quoin – Decorative square or rectangular-shaped blocks that project slightly at the corners of a building, commonly made of stone, brick or stucco.

R

R-value – Measure of the resistance of a material to the passage of energy—the higher the R-value, the greater the insulating capability of the material.

Rafters – Structural components that create the shape of a roof, typically cut and assembled piece by piece on site.

Raised Slab – Flat concrete foundation elevated with concrete blocks or poured walls and filled with compacted dirt before pouring the slab.

Rake – Edge of the roof that runs along the slope.

Rebar – Short for "reinforcing bar." Steel rod used to strengthen concrete and support connections between slabs and other parts of the structure.

Reglet – Slit cut into masonry material, such as a chimney, to allow the installation of flashing.

Ridge – Horizontal line created at the juncture of two sloping roof planes.

Ridge Board – Framing member running along the ridge of the roof. Rafters are nailed to this component.

Ridge Cap – Shingles installed as finish course at the ridge.

Ridge Vent – Vent system installed along the ridge of the roof to provide ventilation for the roof area.

Rise – Vertical distance measured from the base of a stairway to the top, from tread to tread, or from the eave of a roof to the ridge.

Riser – Vertical finish surface of a stair between two treads.

Roof Window – Similar to a skylight, but with an opening sash.

Rough In – Preliminary stage of installation of plumbing, HVAC, electrical wiring, etc., prior to the application of finish surfaces and materials.

Rough Opening – Opening that must be framed in a wall to allow for the installation and shimming of a door, window or other components.

Run – Horizontal distance covered by a stair or roof.

S

Sash – Framework that holds the panes of glass in a window, which moves in a window that opens.

Scale – Mathematical relationship between one thing and another, such as between the architectural drawings and the actual structure itself.

Scissor Truss – Roof truss that creates a cathedral ceiling with an interior slope.

Sconce – Wall-mounted light fixture.

Section Drawing – Architectural drawing that provides a view of the structure or a component as a vertical slice.

SEER Rating – "Seasonal Energy Efficiency Ratio" used to rate the efficiency of cooling equipment.

Shakes – Hand-split wood shingles of varying thickness with an irregular surface.

Sheathing – Various building materials applied to floors, walls and roofs that create the surface for application of finish materials.

Shed Roof – Roof shape with only a single slope, usually attached to the side of a structure.

Sheetrock – A brand of drywall manufactured by U.S. Gypsum, commonly used to describe the material.

Shim – Slim, beveled piece of wood used to fill small spaces in framing and trim, such as around windows and doors.

Shingles – Thin, usually rectangular pieces of material, such as wood, slate or asphalt roofing, overlapped to create a weatherproof layer over a roof or a side wall.

Shiplap – Shape milled into the edge of material, such as wood siding, that allows an edge to overlap another.

Shoe – See "base shoe."

Sill – Horizontal member at the base of windows or the lowest member of the framework of a wall, sometimes called the mudsill.

Sill Plate – Piece of lumber applied over the top edge of a foundation used to secure floor framing above.

Single-hung Window – Window that resembles a double-hung, but only the lower sash is operable.

Sleeper – Wood member resting on a concrete slab, used to support and raise a finished floor.

Soffit – Underside of an overhang at the eaves of a roof or the ceiling bulkhead constructed above cabinets or vanity areas.

Soil-bearing Capacity – Measurement of the ability of a soil to support structural loads from a structure.

Soil Pipe – System of pipes, usually PVC, used to carry water and sewage from the fixtures to the sewer or septic.

Soil Stack – Main vertical plumbing pipe that collects drainage and waste materials from sinks, toilets, tubs and showers.

Sound Attenuation Blanket – Fiberglass insulation-type material used to deaden the transfer of sound through areas of a building.

Span – Horizontal distance between bearing points supporting rafters, trusses and joists.

Splash Block – Flat material, usually concrete or wood, placed on grade below a downspout to direct water away from the building.

Square – Term used to describe the quantity of roofing or siding material needed to cover 100 square feet.

Stakeout – Act of measuring and driving stakes in the ground to indicate the location of a building, driveway, septic system or other improvement prior to excavation and construction.

Steel Door – Another term used to describe metal door.

Stile – Vertical framing members of a paneled door.

Stool – Interior trim sometimes installed at the sill of a window that creates a narrow shelf.

Stringer – Boards at the side of stairs that slope up the wall at an angle.

Stucco – Plaster, made with Portland cement, sand and water, that is sometimes used as an exterior finish. Synthetic stucco, also known as EIFS, is more commonly used in residential and commercial construction today.

Stud – Vertical framing components of a wall, usually a 2x4 spaced 16 inches on center.

Subfloor – First layer of sheathing applied over the joists in a double-layer floor construction.

Sturdi-floor – American Plywood Association designation for a single-layer, glued floor system.

Sump Pump – Pump installed below grade, usually in a basement, to pump ground water up and away from a building.

Suspended ceiling – See "dropped ceiling."

T

Terra Cotta – Reddish-brown, fired clay often used for flowerpots, floor tiles and ornaments.

Terrace – Paved outdoor area, sometimes raised.

Thinset – Mortar-like setting material used for the installation of ceramic tile and marble.

Toenail – Nail driven at an angle to the framing member.

Tongue and Groove – Shape milled into the edge of board that allows for an over-lapping connection, as in T&G flooring.

Topographic Survey – Survey that measures the relative elevations or grades on a site, typically based on the relationship to mean sea level.

Transom – Window installed above other windows or doors.

Trap – U-shaped bend in a drain or waste line that holds a small amount of water to prevent sewer gases from entering the house.

Tray (Trey) Ceiling – Flat ceiling with the center portion raised and the vertical areas surrounding usually sloped.

Tread – Horizontal part of a stair upon which you step.

Treated Wood – See "pressure-treated wood."

Trim – Decorative molding, the act of installing moldings and finish materials.

Truss – Engineered structural component, assembled from wood members, metal connectors, designed to carry structural loads such as in a roof or a floor system.

U

Underlayment – A layer of panel material, such as plywood, installed just below the finish floor.

Utilities – Describes gas, electric, telephone and other such services brought to the building.

V

Valley – Internal angle formed by two sloping planes of a roof.

Vapor Barrier – Paper or plastic material installed directly behind the interior wall finish to prevent moisture from moving through a wall.

Vaulted Ceiling – Ceiling that rises above the wall height with one or more slopes or angles.

Veneer – Thin sheets of wood, such as the layers in a piece of plywood.

Ventilation – Movement of air through roof cavities important to controlling moisture, elimination of stale air from inside the building.

Veranda – Long, covered porch.

Vestibule – Entry foyer.

W

Waferboard – Structural panels manufactured using chips or wafers of wood glued together and sealed, used primarily for floor, wall and roof sheathing.

Wainscot – Wood paneling, usually on the lower part of an interior wall.

Wall Tie – Small corrugated metal strap bent and nailed in place to connect brick and stone fascia to a side wall.

Wallboard – Term usually used to describe drywall.

Waste Pipes – See "soil pipes."

Weep Hole – Small drain holes installed at the base of brick veneer walls to allow moisture to escape.

Wind Load – Measurement calculated by engineers to determine the structural design necessary to stand up to the force of severe weather gales.

Wire Mesh – Metal wire manufactured in a grid work, usually 6" x 6", installed in a concrete slab to minimize the separation of concrete due to cracking and settling.

Wolmanized Wood – Brand name of pressure-treated wood.

Wood Floor System – Floor system constructed of wood framing, including floor joists and floor sheathing, typically suspended over a crawl space, basement or other area of the structure.

Working Drawings – Final version of the architectural drawings approved and used for the actual construction.

Z

Zoned Heating System – System that separates the building into areas, or zones, to allow for separate control of levels of heating and cooling to maximize comfort and energy efficiency.

Made in the USA
Coppell, TX
03 September 2020

35617312R10085